Vague Memories

*A Story about Family Legacy,
Poland and Everyday Moments*

Joanna Puciata

Published by Heal 'N Glow

Printed in the United States of America

Edited by Ellen Stumbo

Cover Design by Alexandra Suh

Library of Congress Control Number: 2012918316

Puciata, Joanna

Vague Memories, A Story about Family Legacy,
Poland and Everyday Moments

Library of Congress Cataloguing-in-Publication Data

ISBN: 9781938579486

❦ Dedication ❦

To my brave and lovely mother, Maria Puciata. You showed us what unconditional love can do. You always put us first, and knowing we were curious children, you magically turned ordinary into extraordinary. This book is a tribute to you and to my sister Kasia, who flourished through your love and had best possible life ever.

To my children, Julian and Marcel Targowski, Noor and Laila El-Shamaa. Be proud of your heritage and never forget the people that shaped you into who you are. You have their talents, their smiles, their temper. You share with them more than you can possibly imagine. Keep them close to your heart and never forget your roots.

To my Egyptian husband, Marwan Shamaa, for loving me despite our enormous cultural differences.

To all my friends who supported me in my writings, especially Karina Kott and Anna Nalls, who cheered me up when I had doubts about my writing capabilities and always believed in me.

To Ellen Stumbo, my editor who showed-up in my life in a God ordianed way. You've lightened my words about my sister because you understood through your own experience what Down Syndrome means. I couldn't have asked for a better person in my wildest dreams.

⚜ You said... ⚜

This draft with memories of Kasia is written well and with great feeling. Is a treaty on LOVE. This is a poem about a HUMAN, about her talents, her beautiful nature and life. At the same time, it is an APPEAL to future mothers not to be afraid!

Maria Puciata, Poland – Kasia's Mom

Your memories from Poland brought special vivid moments of my own past. I actually WAS ON THAT TRAIN to the Baltic Sea (my dad insisted on frequent summer trips to the sea...), and I WAS CHECKING ON THAT CARP in the bathtub before Christmas! (Every year!) I like your choice of events from the past, and how you described them. Your way of writing of the Polish past speaks to me because unlike a lot of Polish people living abroad I have met so far, you are able to deliver appreciation rather than criticism for the life that once was.

Renata Schnelker, USA

I must say even though I do not know your sister Kasia, I felt in a short moment I was able to know who she was as a person. You blew my heart and mind away, it was so touching, and what wonderful work she did. I can relate to some of the moments Kasia had and the experience that she went through. I the way in which you're keeping Kasia's memory alive is wonderful. I truly believe this is the reason God gives us memories: to be able to recall and never forget our loved ones. I want to thank you for sharing your stories with me, it truly means a great deal. It touched me to see pictures of Kasia and I felt your sense of missing this wonderful person that God put in your life. They are angels who are sent to us to make our lives easier through hard times and they have the most beautiful and loving hearts.

Nilda Alfaro, USA

Kasia was my friend. Sometimes, she would call me and ask for my address. She visited only a couple of times but her presence is always with me through her art. The art of a beautiful heart and a deep understanding of the nature of painting. Kasia was not afraid of unexpected color compilations or the quick strokes of a brush. Result: abstract landscapes turned into a journey to Kasia's incredible life. She continues to take me to her dreamy world of both dark and joyful pictures.

Marta Madigan, USA

I applaud your work and admire your talent. Your writing took me back to my beloved neighborhood, and it is such a comforting feeling knowing after all these years I am not the only one remembering it THAT way. Kasia is proud of you!

Dorota Otrebska, Canada

Incredible depth of Kasia's paintings leads my feelings inside her soul. There seems to be an untouchable connection between my own self (the viewer) and Kasia's vision of the world, greater than what we normally can see. I wonder if others can feel and see this mystery of life with the same intensity, or if my own experiences brought me to the place where I can appreciate the unknown so much more than ever before. The beauty of those paintings lies in people's ability to open up their hearts and see the pictures in the light of their interpretation.

Margaret Skrzypkowski, USA

❧ Contents ❧

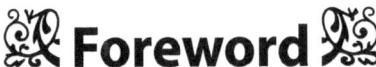 Foreword

Joanna Puciata will take you to a far away land of not too long ago in Warsaw, Poland. The family dynamics and the warmth of their home will make you forget the hardships of a time when the socialistic rule oppressed the Polish people.

The family legacy is simply an example and an encouragement for all to follow. A gentle challenge that whispers, "What are you doing to instill wonder and life in your children?"

Although Vague Memories is a short memoir, it is also a voice that stands out amidst the oppression of the time to show the power of the human spirit, and the power of will to hold on to what makes our hearts beat. Through these pages, you will feel the pure joy and unending love the family shared. This is a tale that will encourage and inspire because of the simplicity of life, yet the richness of spirit.

As a fellow mother of a child with Down syndrome, I found Joanna's accounts of her sister, Kasia, to be especially touching. Evidence that people with Down syndrome have great potential, and a real example of what it means to love your children unconditionally, and encourage them in their talents and gifts.

I wanted to reach across the pages and extend my help and support to her mother, as she had to stand insults and rejection because of her daughter not being what others considered "normal." Kasia's level of independence was a testimony of the dedication and support she had from her family. The love between Kasia and her father was touching.

At the end of the book, I wanted to know this family personally, to sit down and have a cup of Turkish coffee with them, and share more stories about what life was like for them.

Vague Memories is a rare treat, and the message of the story will touch the hearts of its readers.

Ellen Stumbo

I lived in a world that doesn't exist anymore. Born in 1967 in Warsaw, Poland, during socialistic times, I had the fortune of being raised by those brought-up in another system. Through my bedtime stories, the echoes of the leisure and richness of the pre Second World War times came to life through their vivid memories. Through these stories, I experienced the lavish daily breakfasts for twenty, the sumptuous meat roast marinating for days, the

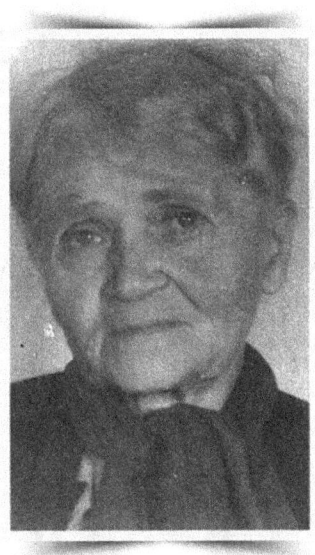

*My Great Grandmother,
Helena Rykaczewska*

eccentricity of an unknown great-grandmother – an aristocrat, yet one of the country's first idealistic social democrats – the wealth of the family, and the Sunday boredom.

Through narratives, I relived the horror of the Second War, the hunger, and the fear of my 8-year-old mother who fled through Warsaw with one suitcase, leaving behind a lifetime of accumulated riches. She found solace at a refugee camp with thousands of other people. She managed to get out due to my grandfather's connections and the family fled to their summer house. The time spent there was no longer idyllic. Nevertheless, it was much better in contrast with the time spent locked-up in her Warsaw home basement, with nothing to eat or drink except for canned sardines and wine. When she returned to a free Warsaw, it was only to face another suppressor, socialism. My grandparents and mother searched for a new house among the Warsaw ruins. However, in a new system where capitalists and aristocrats no longer held status or power, they were forced to give up what was once theirs and search for new identities and goals.

From these tales I could picture the happy fifties and sixties. The elegance of the world of fashion captivated me, along with the fascination with Armstrong, Sinatra and Nat King Cole. I cherished the stories where my parents traveled to colorful worlds in Western Europe or the Middle East, full of different customs, foods, and riches beyond our gray reality.

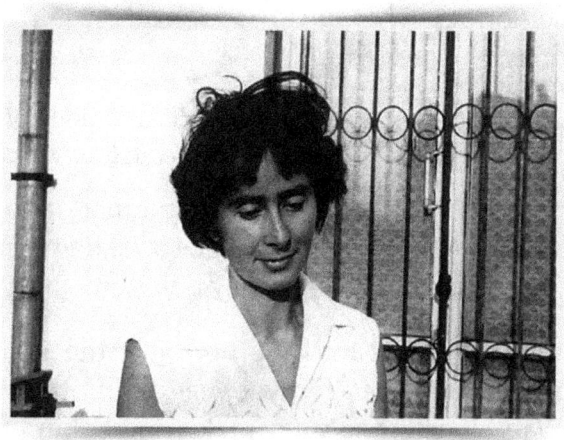

My beautiful mother, Maria Puciata

It wasn't until the mid seventies, when I was about 8 years old, that I realized we were unique from others, but I loved it. Thirty years later, when someone mentioned that my family wasn't "normal", I looked at him amazed and shocked, "But what do you mean by that?"

With rare beauty and elegance – a vestige of our former aristocratic days – we stood out all right! I can imagine the picture of our family walking down the street: a gorgeous woman with a delicate demeanor, high heels and a fitted dress pushing a handsome man on a wheelchair with a Humphrey Bogart hat and a great sense of humor; his elegant, tall brother keeping their pace wearing a suit and a cowboy scarf around his neck; and two children – one with Down Syndrome – all laughing. People turned their heads around amazed by the unusual wave of elegance and lightness brought to their common world. At least, that is how I remember feeling.

I am grateful to God for being brought-up in this fascinating family and during those particular times. I am one of those people who wouldn't change anything from my childhood, for despite the hardships, it was as happy as it gets. My life, somehow, reminds me of one of my favorite movies, "Life is Beautiful" with Roberto Benigni, where life itself wasn't treated too seriously and where love made it an unforgettable adventure.

I offer you these memories of a childhood spent in Poland, where despite disability and loss, we all basked in love and our hearts overflowed.

Enjoy!

Joanna Puciata

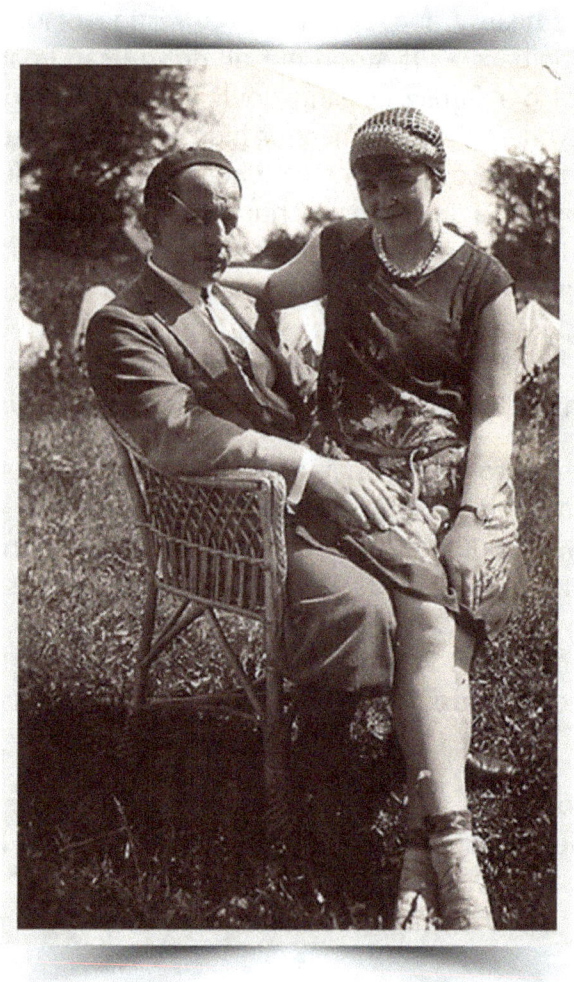

*Maternal Grandparents, Mieczyslaw Matejak
and Maria Rykaczewska*

𝕸 My Parents 𝕸

My mother was born into an aristocratic family in Poland. My grandfather owned a mustard plant located in central Warsaw. The factory survived the German occupation, but gave-in to the new socialist system. They allowed him to keep a job as a general manager, but three years later he was out of a job from the place he once owned.

The government owned everything, and they seemed to punish those who once held wealth and status in the old class system. At the age of twenty, my mom's twin brother, Uncle Maciek, traveled to join the army (which back then was mandatory for all men). Yet, when he arrived at his destination he discovered he was assigned to work in a coal mine to do hard labor for a year. For a year, he worked seven days a week, without any time off. The government wanted to show how weak the wealthy class was, and they succeeded.

My parents met when they were teenagers. They were high school sweethearts, and early on they tackled Poland's life challenges together. They had plans to go to college, because not having a college education was equal to social degradation.

My dad was brilliant, but he never cared for studying. His grades were poor across the board, improving only where my mother helped. Thanks to her, he became an engineer and an expert in heavy machinery operations. My uncle Maciek failed a class and was held back a year. This must have become a motivation for him, because today he is Europe's most renowned expert in wood technology. My mother, on the other hand, loved to study. Unfortunately, she failed her first attempt to get into the university by writing down on a form that her father was an industrialist, not a working class parent. My poor mother wanted to be an art historian, but because she was rejected to that program, she had to apply to become an engineer just to have a degree. All three graduated with the same degree in wood technology.

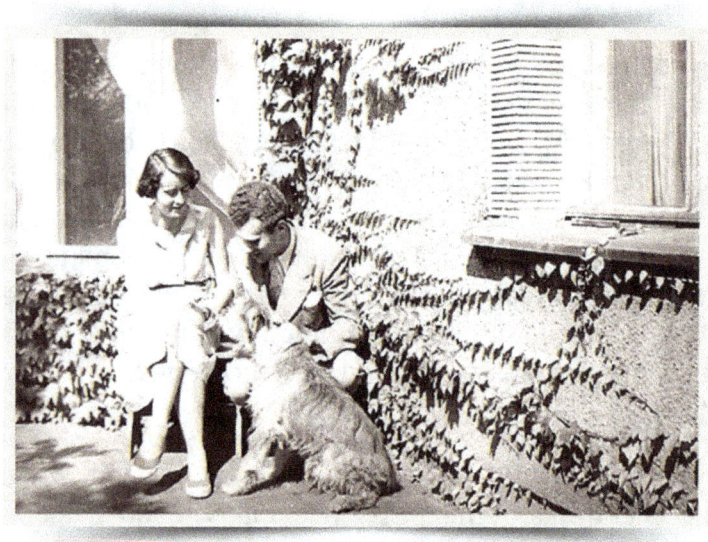

My father was full of jokes and mischief; he never cared much for money, spending it frivolously on whatever he desired. Both of my parents traveled abroad for work. My mom ate

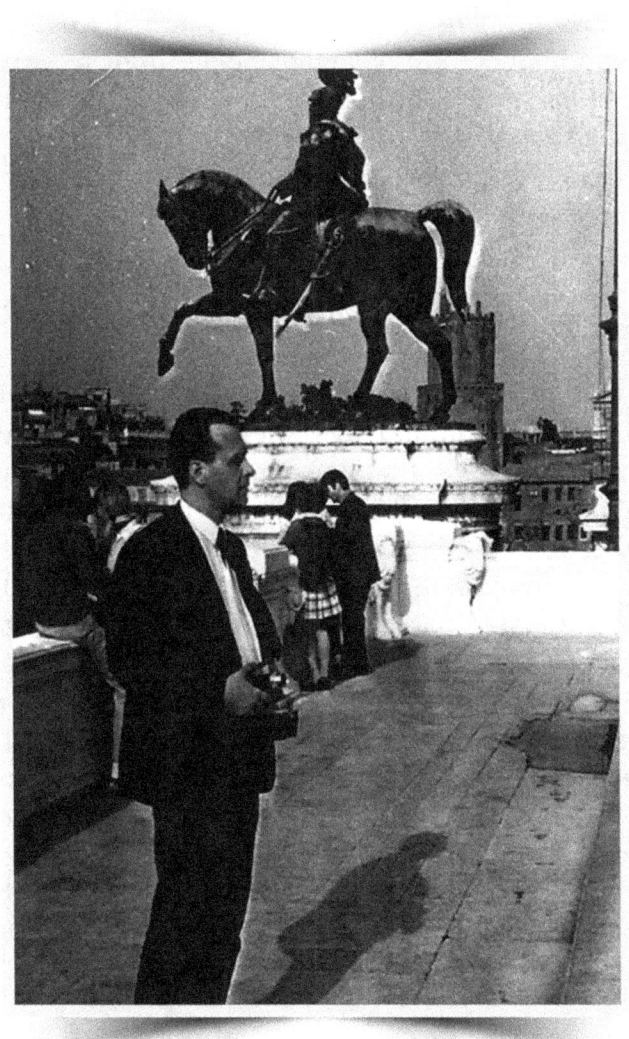

My elegant father, Jacek Puciata, in Rome

only one small meal a day and saved every extra penny that her job provided for food allowance in order to bring the most dollars home where they had huge value. My dad, on the other hand, spent most of it enjoying life, drinking expensive wines, eating exotic foods, and often spending all his earnings on beautiful dresses for my mom. My mom got mad, but could never change the way he was. He must have known he wasn't going to live long, and subconsciously made the best out of the short life he was given.

I was seven years old when dad came home from work early and said his legs hurt. I knew in my childish mind that it was a defining moment, as it stuck with me forever. He was soon diagnosed with Multiple Sclerosis, a disease for which there was no cure. He tried everything, from medication, to rehabilitation, to healers. I particularly remember a Russian healer. He came to Warsaw once in a while and his presence alone brought us great hope. He held dad's head in his hands, performing some energy healing. Each time, my dad was sure he'd walk back home on his own two legs. Together, dad and I imagined the moment he would stand up and leave the wheelchair behind. I would prepare his nicest clothes; the suit or a yellow knitted sweater with a scarf, a hat and a cane (as a sign of a great aristocrat, not an illness). We imagined walking together down the street, me holding on to his arm, him scaring away all the men looking at his beautiful daughter. We never had this moment, it remained in our dreams forever, but we could both feel how it would be.

He was a musician by heart. He could barely read notes but he could play anything he heard once. He was a smoker, a joker, and a bon-vivant, as we used to say. Women were crazy about him. But the same was true for my mom, men were crazy about her! Together they were the most beautiful and elegant couple, a husband and wife full of love. The last words he spoke quietly to my mom's ear were "I love you!" He passed away at the age of 46, when I was only twelve years old.

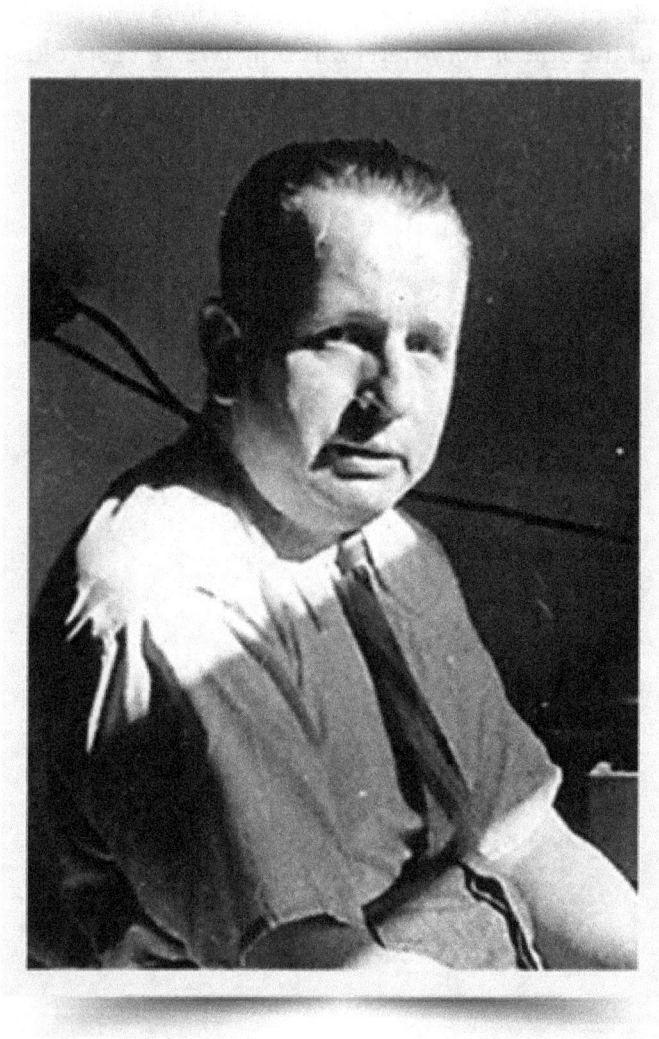

Grandfather, Mieczyslaw Matejak

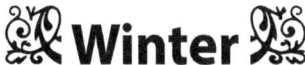 Winter

My sister Kasia and I woke up to an embracing silence, the kind where you can hear your own heartbeat, and you can hear the walls breathe around you. The streets below were quiet, as if the cars drove on a soft Persian rug. Although we were just children, we knew winter had arrived and it had snowed all night.

We walked into the living room, enchanted by the flower designs Jack the Frost painted on our poorly insulated windows. It was 1978 and full-blown socialism ruled our country. The heat in the house was low according to regulations. Nonetheless, without warning, the temperature could drop or the heating stop altogether.

I remember what we referred to as the "Winter of the Century". The snow mountains on the streets were humongous, inviting the children to climb them. The temperatures reached minus thirty degrees Celsius, so one could not stay on the streets for too long. We couldn't walk without covering our faces, or our nasal passages would freeze. The sheep-skin coats and hats – although not very fashionable – kept us all warm. They were very heavy, often reaching our ankles, but we didn't care about looks, only comfort from the chill.

That winter, my grandfather – who was already losing his

memory – decided to walk to our house wearing only a suit and a scarf. He walked for half an hour, trying to remember which building was ours. It was only pure coincidence that my friend's mother, who stopped by for a visit, left our house and ran into my grandfather. She brought him to us half frozen, but smiling like a child. We thought he would die from the cold, but God had a different plan for him. He died the following year; sound asleep in the quiet of his own house.

During the coldest days of that particular Winter, we tried to stay warm by moving the beds into our kitchen. The only heat source in the house was the open kitchen oven and the burning stove flames. It was not much, but without it, it would be impossible to stay alive in the cold. We slept in heavy sweaters, hats and socks under at least two covers. Baths were highly improvised. Once in a while we partially scrubbed our bodies with a sponge. First the top half, which made us shiver uncontrollably, then the rest after we put sweaters on. We watched American movies, where every room had warm rugs and warm walls. Even though we lived in the capital of the centrally located European country, we felt like an abandoned and forgotten tribe.

When the temperature was bearable, my sister and I played outside; we'd go sledding to a nearby park until our socks were wet and freezing. Or we'd go by the school where every winter our janitor poured water into the field creating an outdoor ice arena. We memorized every centimeter of the ice surface. We knew exactly which areas were slippery, which ones had bubbly bumps, and which ones were over the dirt. The modern ice arenas with clean ice and loud music paled in comparison to the "homemade" one we had, with the moon lighting up the scenery, the dark shadows of the trees, and the sound of cars passing by. We spent hours fooling around until frostbite or hunger forced us to go home. Frozen wool socks and gloves hung off the radiators, while hot soup and hot tea warmed us from the inside. Sometimes, when our hands itched too much and our fingers were too stiff to hold the spoon, we soaked them in warm water, even though we knew that frozen hands should go in cold water.

🕸 Joy of Christmas 🕸

A few weeks before Christmas time, we started making decorations. We cut circles out of colored paper and glued them together to form a thick stack of many layers. Our favorite was a bomb, made out of paper maché and held together by a thread in the middle. Once we had enough circles glued together to form a sort of ball, we cut incisions around the edges to make a fluffy ball. All the children loved this one, but it took a lot of work.

The food preparations began many weeks before Christmas. Due to the shortages of food, everyone seemed to need the same ingredients at the same time for our traditional meal. Even though the Roman Catholic tradition did not allow meat on Christmas Eve, we had all sorts of meat the following days. Since Polish refrigerators were very small, people hung their meats from the flower hooks outside their windows. It was common to see a whole rabbit hanging by the feet waiting for its turn to be skinned and made into a paté, or some sort of game hen waiting to be defeathered and served on a silver platter as part of old Polish tradition. When food became even scarcer, those who hung their bags with food or wild game outside, especially those living on the lower floors took the risk of losing their food to thieves. I always turned my head avoiding the view from the windows and vowed never to eat the chickens, along with other types of meat.

I loved the times when a peasant woman knocked on our door. She carried a bucket of fresh sour cream, which she ladled into our own glass jars, or fresh eggs with pieces of feathers or hay still attached to the shells, and fresh produce. I loved the look of the farmer's cheese with imprints of the cheesecloth. The woman's bruised hands, stained with dark unwashable lines, worked effectively as she cut a piece or two for my mother. She carried the heavy bucket, bags and aluminum milk jar from floor to floor hoping to go back home with an empty container and coins in her pocket.

We stood in long lines trying to buy flour, poppy seeds for the cake, fish, meat and eggs. Once we had the poppy seeds, our whole family participated in the meticulous process of simmering them in milk for hours and grinding them several times into a whitish paste. It was usually a man's job to grind the poppy seeds, as it required some strength. Everything we had was manual, from the washer to the eggbeater on a wooden stick. But there would be no Christmas without the poppy seed cake, and no matter how long we had to beat the egg whites or knead the dough or grind the seeds, it had to be done.

Fish preparation was an elaborate process. It had to be fresh and alive until the last minute. Therefore, a few days before Christmas we woke up to one or two fishes swimming in our bathtub. For a child, it was surreal. When the fish were ready to cook, my nanny – who lived with us until I was 8 – put salt by their fins where the fish breathed and said they died a peaceful death. She boiled their heads with vegetables to form a gelatinized liquid. The sauce was then poured over the cooked fish, which was decorated with green peas, carrots, eggs and parsley. It was usually the centerpiece of the table. The other fish was served hot with an almond sauce, next to the boiled potatoes. For us children, the best part of fish cooking was goofing off with the cleaned fish intestines that resembled long white balloons. We didn't have many toys and tried to find joy in the ordinary things.

No Christmas Eve feast at my house came without herring varieties, served with oil and onion, or sour cream and lemon. The taste of the hot potatoes with butter and dill next to the cold herring in sour cream and lemon sauce with crunchy onions was mouth watering. (Even now, after my eating habits have changed dramatically, I drool over the memory and allow myself to indulge in it once a year at my friend Zb's house, despite my husband's terrified look.)

We considered ourselves lucky, living above the most famous Warsaw Kalasa bakery. Getting bread was the least difficult task of all. On Christmas Eve, people from distant parts of Warsaw waited in line for hours in order to make it in. But my sister, who was well known in the neighborhood and had Down syndrome, was served first, along with war veterans and pregnant women. The smell of fresh bread coming out of the bakery could knock you down on your knees. There was a time when I was very little, when the anti-Semitic socialist system somehow overlooked the great Jewish tradition of baking challah on Friday evenings in preparations for the Shabbat. Our bakery was famous for it and was selling them hot, straight from the oven. The crust was golden and had plenty of irresistibly sweet crumbs that all the children picked with their fingers. No challah or French baguette ever made it home intact.

A few days before Christmas Eve, our father took us to the market to buy a Christmas tree. The whole place was lit-up with white bulbs and smelled like a forest. I loved the small booths filled with handmade ornaments, so colorful and sparkly. Our daily lives, from clothes, to cosmetics, to wall color were quite dull; therefore seeing such richness in color was elevating. I wanted them all, but I never made a fuss over not getting more and was happy with what we got.

My dad picked the tree; not too tall, quite modest. It had plenty of spaces between the branches, so that all the ornaments would show. We dragged it home over the crunchy snow and struggled setting it in the stand. Before electric tree bulbs became available to us due to the socialist reign, we used little golden clips with thin candles. The moment the electric tree lights were available in our stores, we bought them. I remember the story from before I was born, when my father, who had plenty of artistic ideas, decided to decorate the room walls with hay. The flame from the candles somehow caught the hay on fire. Luckily, it was quickly put down.

On Christmas Eve, my mom cooked almost until the end of the day. My job was to polish the silverware, wash the old plates and set-up the table. The silver was old and heavy, it had been passed down from generation to generation in the family. Some utensils had engraved royal crowns; some had my uncle's initials. I'd polish each fork, knife and spoon with toothpaste until my hands were clay gray. I spread out a dark blue tablecloth with rich fringes and golden Arabic designs embroidered all over, something my father brought from Syria, and went against the Polish tradition of rigid, white, starchy tablecloths.

My mother transformed herself from Cinderella to a princess within minutes of the first star appearing on the sky, indication of the beginning of the Christmas Eve supper. She'd brush off the fatigue from her face, replacing it with light blue eye shadow, backcombed hair, pink lipstick, and high heeled shoes. I admired her will to make any holiday or reception perfect, and to make an eternal impression on the guests. She always looked elegant in her clear stockings and colorful necklaces. The sound of her high heels touching the hardwood floor echoed around the room. We sat down for supper feeling majestic. My mom kissed everyone, whispering special wishes for each one of us. We engaged in formal conversation, indulging in all the food served on porcelain platters.

I loved it when my dad's brother , Olgierd, came over with his wife Maja. Both eloquent, theatrical, brilliant and majestic. They brought life and light to any gathering. Maja always wore thin nylons, high heels and red lipstick. She was brought-up at Sacre Coeur de Versaille in France, and entertained us for hours with her stories. Olgierd always wore a suit and a cowboy scarf around his neck. He sat back on a chair with his legs crossed, holding a pipe in one hand and making vivid gestures with the other. He was tall and big, and spoke in a fascinating deep tone. They were both art historians, interesting, intriguing, and well-mannered people. And they always brought oranges with them as presents for us! An orange was a luxury at the time.

Presents came last; Christmas was more about spiritual connection than about commercial joy. We got what was available. As ordinary as the gifts seemed to be, they gave us real joy; books, nice chocolates, a toy when we were younger, a music record – either classical or pop. The only time we got spoiled was when I was very little. Mom took my sister and me to the kitchen. After a moment, my dad called us to the living room. We only had two rooms, divided by a huge wooden double door with black metal hinges. (The door was a subject of everyone's envy, made to order by one of my mom's friendly manufactures, and causing exclamations in the gray world of simplicity and commonness.) We stood by the door, feeling the cold air coming from the gap between the door and the floor. Then we heard my father's voice inviting us inside the room. The door opened wide and what we saw stayed with me forever: toys aligned by the wall, lots and lots – or so it seemed – a wide open window and traces of snow on the floor and my father waving goodbye to Santa Claus, thanking him for stopping by. It was a most memorable experience that happened only once.

One winter, however, I was able to get a present for my mother. When she got frostbite from walking in her worn out shoes to my French lesson, I got lucky enough to buy her a new pair of shoes. It didn't matter that I bought her men's boots. I happened to be next to the shoe store when there was a delivery and a line formed immediately. Nobody was asking what kind of delivery there was; instead everybody was happy to have a chance of buying any kind of shoe. The boots didn't wait to be put under the tree, I gave them to my mom as soon as we got home from my lesson and they lasted for many years.

Over the years, the number of table settings for our Christmas Eve celebration shrunk, but my mother never seized to impress. She made sure the table was properly set, with neatly folded napkins, and there were extra settings to remember the loved ones who left us in this world, or for the stranger who might knock at the door.

After Christmas, the parties and big celebrations began, starting with official brunches. The first one always hosted by my aunt's next door neighbor. We called my aunt "Old Lala" to distinguish between her and her daughter "Little Lala." Old Lala was a descendant of the great Genghis Khan. My family had roots in Russia, but we are uncertain how this man came to the family. As a child, I was fascinated by this fact and looked upon my flirtatious aunt with admiration. She had a beautiful smile that reflected in the twinkling of her eyes. For as long as I can remember, she wore light blue eye shadow and smelled of strong perfume. She was extremely animated and loved to gossip in a theatrical way. When her daughter, Little Lala, got pregnant, she whispered the fact to my mom's ear, but then told her out loud not to mention "anything about *that butter!*" I was dying of curiosity about the "butter" and forced my mom to tell me everything. My cousin, who is now a great violoncellist, was born the day after my father passed away.

Aunt Lala was a very powerful and strong-willed woman. Her husband lived in her shadow and cried like a child when she died. She wasted away to cancer, and even now I am terrified when someone loses weight too quickly. Brunches at her house were always remarkable and never boring. Her living room consisted of a bed, a big old mahogany closet with a dusty mirror, a piano, a beauty chest with cosmetics and a round table covered with a flowery tablecloth. The chairs were heavy and gave me a sense of stability. We sat for hours listening to the adult conversations and eating till we could breathe no more.

Soon after, the New Year preparations began. When my dad

– who at age 39 suffered from Multiple Sclerosis and was unable to walk – was still in good health, he threw parties like no one else. It was the time of Luis Armstrong, Banana Boat Song as well as rock and roll, twist and cha-cha. Crowds of as many as forty gathered in our small apartment. We pushed the furniture and rugs to the walls and danced. My father was well known for his impressive entertainment ideas. My mom prepared several chickens and placed them on an enormous copper pan. My father sprinkled them with alcohol, lit them up and brought them into the living room to screams of exclamations and admiration.

New Year celebrations marked the beginning of a Carnival. It was the time to break up the winter boredom. The Carnival would last until Lent and end by what we called a Fat Thursday, where the whole country was buying paczki, a kind of doughnut with white glaze and jam inside. These donuts were the favorite among children, and although other countries have tried to duplicate them, there is nothing like the original Polish donuts. They are popular in the US Polish stores, but nowhere near the shape or taste of the ones from my childhood.

☙ Vacations ❧

Late January meant we had a winter break. Every year our family retreated to the mountains during winter and spring breaks and to the Baltic Sea or the lakes during summer. It was an ardent task to get a place on a train, as they were usually booked beyond capacity and were often a cause of great disputes. There were a few times when seats weren't assigned, creating chaos at the train station, and Darwinism, with its survival of the fittest, was displayed in its purest form. The strongest, with the lightest luggage (usually men), were able to get into the slowly moving train by jumping through the windows. Those wishing to enter in a civilized manner through the doors often had to spend the night in the hallway, considering themselves lucky if they found one of the seats built on the wall available. Hallways weren't heated and if somebody wanted to smoke and open the window they did it at any time without any consideration of others. One time, I developed pneumonia because of this. Most of the time, however, we did have assigned seats and we traveled with some comfort. Second class consisted of eight seats making us curious about whom we would be traveling with, hoping there were no drunk people in the cabin.

My mom made friends easily and always struck interesting conversations, making others tell her their life stories, express their political views, or share their tea with us. Most people brought their own food along for the ride. Cheese sandwiches, hard-boiled eggs and hot tea in a thermos were what most people carried with them. There was a diner wagon called "Wars." To get there, one had to cross the wagons and all the children were afraid of doing this. A shaky, harmonica like stretchy rubber connected the wagons. Every step felt as if you were about to fall into the hole in the floor and straight under the running train. My sister despised anything moving and always made an embarrassing scene around the escalators and train connections. She loved to eat, and would jump at any opportunity to have a meal or a cup of coffee. But she was terrified of the train's passage, making a big deal about it. Therefore, we always tried to avoid going to the diner on the train. My sister never liked drunks either, and we tried to stay away from places where they served beer. She made strong comments out loud, pointing at drunk people and laughingly saying, "Oh, drunk!" Often offering them a "kick in the butt." For our sake they could not always understand what she was saying, we had to pull her by the hand, often covering her with our arms and rushing through the area, begging her not to make a scene. She was so aware of the differences yet so innocent. But she hated drunks and was very honest expressing her opinion about them.

Once in the mountains, any inconvenience of the travel was forgotten. The fresh cold mountain air revived us immediately. The ride to the house or resort was often breathtaking, especially if it involved a sled with horses, a popular means of transportation in the Zakopane region. It always seemed as if we were somewhere abroad. People spoke a different dialect and it seemed funny to us, the capital people. Men often wore the heavy and stiff wool pants embroidered on the sides with beautiful designs, a sheepskin coat or a vest, and a black wool hat. They were vibrant and different from us, seeming so colorful. Women usually wore their traditional dresses during special occasions, but a lot of them wore black and red flowery scarves on a daily basis.

The house we stayed in had several bedrooms and a common bathroom. There were no luxuries but everything was sparkling clean and inviting. The light pinewood walls and floors added a feeling of warmth to the room. Crispy clean and starchy white bed covers and white curtains welcomed us to a home away from home. Unlike today, when we tend to go a hundred miles per hour even during our time off, or go on vacation packages jam-packed with exciting things, visiting seven countries in seven days. Instead, our vacations were quite long, two or three weeks in one spot. We forgot about the world we came from and were able to slow down and relax. We were always supplied full meals on schedule. Sometimes, a nearby house served the food, but it was always included in our accommodations.

No matter which region of Poland we were, breakfast consisted of hot milk cereal served in a deep vase with a ladle, rye bread, small squares of butter, some jam and a platter of cheese or sometimes cold cuts. Supper was usually a repetition of breakfast excluding the cereal. The main meal came around one o'clock in the afternoon, with servings of soup, a main course, and a dessert. Always predictable, with some surprise elements, like the cold cuts, which were scarce around the whole country. Our days revolved around meals, walks, and mountain trips. The small towns were full of tourists and exciting to visit. My mom made sure we had plenty to read after dark and signed us up at the local library upon arrival.

Resort areas had medical and spa services widely available to everyone who had seen the local doctor. While I bathed in a copper tub filled with bubbly mineral water, my mom went for something more drastic, like hot/cold showers. She had to get naked and a lady hosed her down with a very strong current of water to get the cellulite moving. It was a painful, yet highly rejuvenating procedure.

Small shops and souvenir stores filled with wooden statues, local art, embroidered napkins and tablecloths added to the charm of the villages. The smell of crisp air mixed with luscious hot chocolates, dense black coffees, sweets, grilled sausages and smoke coming out of their chimneys was the smell of vacation and bliss, often leaving us light headed for the first couple of days.

Some of those mountain towns were (and still are) famous for their natural mineral water sources. Every type of water had a different medical property, treating anything from kidney stones, to indigestion, to minor aches. They served the water in porcelain cups with a side straw inside buildings that resembled pretty greenhouses. You had to sip it slowly while walking around. Most of the water tasted a bit salty, some had a strong odor of rotten eggs due to the high content of sulfur. I never got myself to drink this one, although I tried it several times (thirty years later I can still taste it in my mouth). We had to drink the water three times a day, usually before meals. It was a nice social event, and gave people a reason to walk to town.

Sometimes we traveled abroad. Going to a different country from a socialistic rule was difficult, especially traveling to the Western World where capitalism ruled. Nevertheless, some people were able to obtain their Visas to travel. I loved going to East Germany with my mom. Berlin represented a different world, clean and modern. It was our hub for transferring to other places. My favorite were the Hartz mountains. They had small, clean towns, with shiny windows, white curtains and flowers in pots. Even the air seemed different and people calmer. Stores had a lot more to offer, from food to school supplies, chamomile tea, and Nivea cream in metal tins. I never felt hatred towards the Germans, even though I lost my great grandmother, my great uncle, and my aunt due to war. From a very young age we relieved the horrors of World War II by watching all the horrific documentaries from concentrations camps. The past was kept alive through stories, so it wouldn't be forgotten and most importantly, never repeated. Nonetheless, events from the past never stopped us from being open minded and curious. My mom's twin brother, uncle Maciek, married a German, and we'd go to Germany as often as we could, loving their simple and organized way of living. One of my favorite memories comes from "Bad Schandau," a spa town down South. We spent evenings at the poolside and sauna filled with eucalyptus oil laden into hot charcoals. Afterwards, we scrubbed our bodies and the braves ones hopped into the ice-cold water to cool off. We'd go to museums, the Dresden Gallery, or caves filled with stalagmites and stalactites. Yet, the things I remember the most are the excellent foods and saunas.

I loved coming home and the moment of opening our door with five different and heavy keys, pushing it wide open and allowing the home to embrace us as if it really missed us. After a long absence, it had a different sound; we could really hear the squeaky wooden floors and the heaviness of the walls; things we never paid attention to on a daily basis. We hurried to open the windows and water the plants, although if we arrived in the evening, my mom postponed these chores until the next morning, saying that the plants were sleeping. She always treated them as if they were alive, pumping them with protein infused water used to soak the meats. She insisted the plants loved it and grew like baobab trees. Having green plants at home cheered the house, but as with everything else, my mom took it to the next step.

When I was around ten, my mom got this wild idea (for the times we lived in it was pretty wild) to go to Prague for a day. She picked me up from summer camp on a Friday morning and we hopped on a train to Prague without any plans, without knowing where we'd stay for the night. On our way out of the train, my mom approached a Polish-speaking couple and asked them if they could help us find a place to sleep. The man worked in Prague as a contractor and rented us his barrack located at the construction site on the outskirts of Prague. It all looked fine during the day, but when we came back at night and were the only ones in the sand filled terrain next to bulldozers and heavy machinery, we were scared. We showered in a hurry, thinking about what would happen if anybody walked into the men's bathroom and found us there. We were so relieved to wake up in the morning alive. We rushed out of the barrack and ran happily to the bus to see the famous main street; Václavské náměstí, and the Hradčany castle. We dined at an expensive restaurant to test my dining skills, to learn the correct alignment of silverware and which one to use for what, in case it was needed in the future. My mom always taught me the old way of living, so that I'd never forget my background, feel intimidated, and so that I would always hold my chest up high. Eating in fancy public places was a test of my skills. These things don't seem to matter anymore, but they were the bridge between who we were and who we had to become. It was a clash of the systems, identities and values.

The only other country I was able to visit with my mom was Sweden. She had a friend there who married a Swedish gentleman and we got invited twice to visit this lovely, peaceful country. Everywhere we went it seemed people were much calmer in comparison to Polish people, who were always frantically trying to find food, toiletries, clothes and every day staples. For my mom, Sweden was the ideal country to live in due to the social care they offered to their handicapped people. When tensions rose in Poland in 1980, my mom gathered all her jewelry, determined to stay in Sweden if the Soviet army were to intervene in our internal fights for freedom. The Solidarity movement was becoming unstoppable, and we were expecting an invasion at any time, knowing well that president Reagan wouldn't do anything to help us. But as nothing happened during our stay, we came back only to face martial law that would put a stop to international travels for a while. My next trip abroad did not take place again until 1982, when I traveled to Hungary with my school. By then, Polish people were beginning to flee the country through refugee camps in Austria and West Germany. Although we contemplated this many times, we never had the courage or will to leave. Our home was like our fortress, our safe place, and we were unable to walk away from our life. And although life seemed hard at times, it was still ours.

🕸 Our house 🕸

Our house was small, about 770 square feet, located in the very heart of Warsaw. Yet, compared to what others had, our house seemed big. During the times of socialism and realism dominating the architecture, our house stood out by having two vast rooms, with open space, big windows, and a decent hallway.

The modern houses were half the square footage of what we had. They looked and felt like miniature dollhouses, with tiny spaces, and even tinier kitchens. Three-bedroom apartments were a luxury, and the living room was part of the bedroom count. They all looked the same. People made jokes about mistakenly walking into a different floor, being able to open the door to somebody else's apartment, and walking into the exact same furniture, layout, and decorations. Unstylish mass production ruled the country resulting in very simple and shiny tables, wall units, and unattractive reclining sofas and chairs.

Our house had none of that. Our home had two big and sunny rooms totaling all of 480 square feet, connected by gorgeous wooden doors. The beautiful, living antiques that filled our home had souls and stories to tell. We were lucky to have Grandma's desk, heavy armoires with squeaky doors, china cabinets with shaky glass, chests with secret drawers and big mahogany tables with sculptured legs and delicate wooden patterns. Many of these antiques survived the greed of war and came from my grandparent's homes, while we gained others from antique stores. Sometimes, when I opened the porcelain cabinet, I could inhale the stale air of the past. The door always made a squeaky sound and I had to hold the cabinet in fear of the glass breaking. (Till this day, I love sipping tea from my grandmother's tea cups and use the silver daily to keep me connected to my roots).

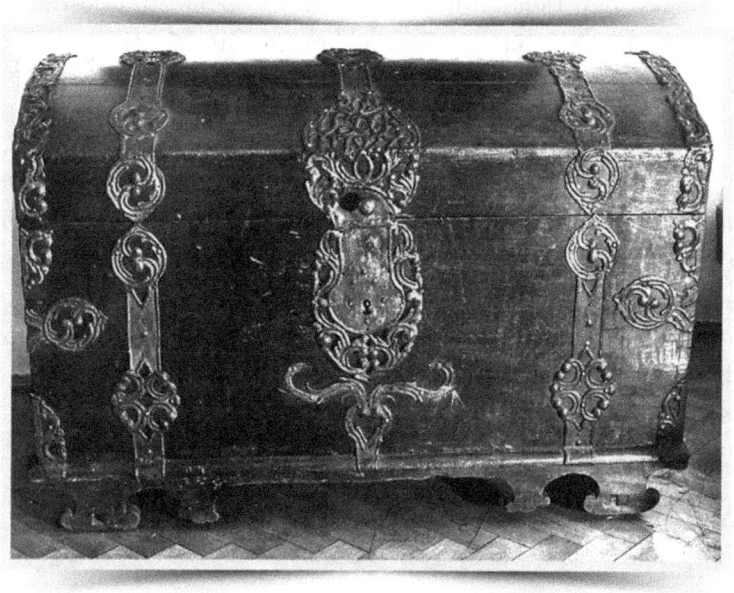

XVII Century chest, our favorite play place, full of hidden treasure

When I was about seven years old, my parents hired a man to restore the furniture to its original beauty. He was a very old man, with wrinkled hands and purple fingernails. His job was to polish the wood by using a round cloth saturated in denatured alcohol. He worked in circular motions caressing the piece he was working on for hours with devoted attention. He fixed the keyholes and repaired any imperfections, making sure to match the era of the furniture. My job was to serve him Turkish coffee, which we all drank from the small mugs my father brought from Istanbul. Watching him work was like watching an artist's performance. He was probably the last of his kind, taking with him the profession that ceased to exist in the following decade, replaced by furniture cleaners. With him gone, my dad passing away, and me moving to America, there was no longer a need for all the mirrors, tables and armoires. My mother sold them, along with some of Napoleon's swords (still seems surreal we possessed some of them), valuable guns, and a huge wooden chest with metal ornaments dating back to the XV century.

The war and the totalitarian system stripped us of any wealth we had left, leaving us with only a few pieces of fine jewelry and some paintings. We hid the jewels in the secret places under the table leg, or behind the double wall, or the armoire to hide the jewelry. As children, we loved when our mom allowed us to awe at grandmother's rings, necklaces and bracelets. We knew where they hid, but we never said a word to anybody. Out of the whole collection of twenty-seven valued paintings that my great uncle possessed before the second war, only two were left – a Rubens and Hornhorst, both dating back to the XV century, divided between my mom and her twin brother. The rest vanished, taken by the German soldiers. One day, my mom declared she was taking our Hornhorst for restoration. She and her brother carried it through the dark alleys and courts under the night sky, in order to avoid being seen or questioned. If the militia found them, they could accuse them of steeling the paining, and they had no proof of ownership. The only superstition's my mother had were about black cats and spiders, so when they ran into a black cat that crossed their path in one of the alleys, my mom decided to risk being caught with the painting by walking around for a block, making sure the cat's path and her path didn't cross each other.

The restoration took a year or maybe two, but with the finest results. At night, I stared at it before falling asleep, reviving the man and the woman flirting with each other, moving, smiling, warming up with a candle. My great uncle Ireneusz Rykaczewski bought this particular painting from a man named Pech, who somehow escaped the Soviet Revolution of 1918 and brought Gerrit Von Hornhorst's painting – cut out of the frame – to Poland. It belonged to the dukes of Dolgorukyi, the founders of Moscow. (Until today, the painting is in our possession and hangs proudly in the same place, above what used to be my bed).

The jewelry and gold became the means of support when times were tough. My sister got sick a lot, and one ring or bracelet covered her medical expenses. We even had my grandmother's golden tooth saved in a box for the "black hour". It disappeared one day, maybe to cover my trip to America in 1986, when I decided to spend a month visiting my high-school sweetheart, who came to Kalamazoo, Michigan to study computer sciences at Western Michigan University. That month turned into twenty-six years. (God bless you grandma!).

Although our kitchen was small, it was large in comparison to what most people had in Warsaw. My father – who was always very inventive – decided to put a wall in the middle of the kitchen in order to divide it and create an extra room for our housekeeper. She was only sixteen when she came to us and stayed for over ten years. At some point she married, and the tiny room she had was a home to her husband and a baby girl. This arrangement didn't last long and they eventually moved out, but it was hard to find your own place, not to mention to buy one. People waited and waited for years, and often decades, to get their own apartment. Until then, most people usually lived with their parents, creating multigenerational families.

Our kitchen then seemed tiny and somewhat dark, but the dividing wall had windows by the ceiling for the sunlight. I used to climb the counter-top and peak through it, sometimes hanging with one leg in the housekeeper's room and the other in the kitchen. Thick wallpaper resembling red brick covered the dividing wall, something my mom brought from her foreign trips. It was a different pattern, warm and inviting. The corners of the kitchen had bunches of dry red hot chili peppers brought in from the neighboring Hungary, wreaths of garlic and dried corn, reminiscence of the big world of color, taste and spices existing mostly in the memories of the few lucky ones.

Since my mother had a degree in wood technology and worked for an exporting company, she had access to small producers of willow and wooden products. She arranged to install a wooden counter-top, fitting the length of the wall. It was unusual then to have something made to order, especially in the big city of Warsaw. We were unique in every aspect of our lives. Once in a while, Ala, the housekeeper, splashed bleach over the counter-top to disinfect it. The countertop served for some heavy cooking, as everything had to be made from scratch. There were no pre-cut pieces of meat available in the stores, and the shortage of basic staples, like noodles, made us make our own. My mom and Ala rolled out the dough and let it hang loosely over the countertop, sprinkled with flour. When semi-dry, the dough was rolled in and cut with a sharp knife into thin strips, which again were left to dry. I loved separating the long strips of dough letting them run through my fingers.

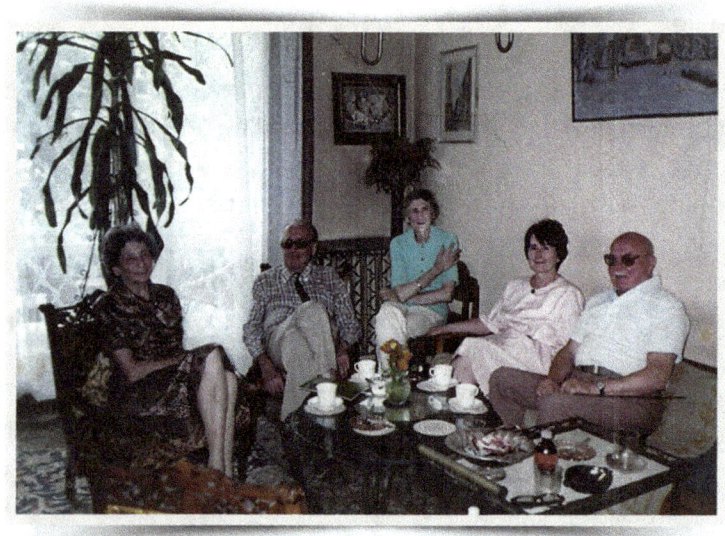

From left, my aunts and my dad's brother Olgierd, my mom and my uncle who loved hunting

Not everything was so pleasant. I never wanted to look at the meat, I despised the look of raw chicken liver, but loved the taste of it, especially when loaded with golden onion. I never, ever approached the kitchen when my mother and Ala made the rabbit paté. The day my parents brought in a wild hen and I had to help my mom pull the feathers out of the poor bird was when I vowed never to taste it, or anything else wild and hunted. Once, my uncle invited us to his Villa on the outskirts of Warsaw. He was a hunter and had two scary looking dogs. He also had the powerful demeanor of a great aristocrat. He was bold, carried a whip in his hand and wore horse pants with tall boots when hunting.

After tea, he asked if we would like to sample some of his delicacies. I wanted to say no, but I knew I was expected to try it. I don't suppose I looked that proper when I forced myself to put the forest smelling pieces of meat in my mouth, chewed it as to not create too much saliva, and spit it out on a napkin, hiding it underneath the teacup. I was terrified, making my move when no one was looking. This was one of the last memories of my uncle, who developed cancer in the 1990's, a diagnosis considered a death sentence back then. Being a "manly" man, he used one of his riffles to shoot himself in the bedroom, spearing himself the humiliation of wasting away.

Our kitchen was a place of secret gatherings with our father. He suffered from Multiple Sclerosis, and at the age of thirty-nine he had to quit his job. When mom was at work, he created a magical experience for us in the kitchen. We cooked, played with pots and pans, recorded music sessions on tape, we drank Turkish coffee and even performed plays! Unable to turn around in his wheelchair in the small space, he made us do the work under his watchful eyes. We soaked almonds in hot water, removed the skins and buried them in salt before baking them in the oven. We made Kogiel Mogiel, a simple dessert made of egg yolks and sugar mixed together with a spoon until it turned pale in color. Then my dad added a secret ingredient, kept even from my mother: a few drops of wine in order to add some zest. Sometimes we added raw cocoa if we felt like chocolate.

My sister and I tasted mussels and other strange delicacies brought from foreign trips. Although these were not children's foods, our parents expected us to try at least one bite. My dad used to tell us not to judge a food by its appearance, but to wait until we tasted it in our mouth. Even when I didn't want to try something, my father was charming, and he had a way with me of creating magic around food as if it were a special treat. I tried radishes with butter and some salt, or even a raw egg for a good soprano voice. I must admit, the egg didn't stay in my mouth and I never developed that great voice, but nevertheless I tried it. A grated apple sprinkled with sugar was a much tastier snack.

Small black and white tiles covered the kitchen floor. It was my mom's dream to change it one day, but tiles weren't available and we had to wait. One day, as I ran downstairs to greet my mother, who was returning from a business trip to London, I saw a city bus pull into our narrow street. My mom stood next to the driver, holding a tall roll of linoleum. She was wearing a sheepskin coat, a skirt, and a flirtatious hat. So feminine, so full of light, and yet looking like a hunter, proud of her conquer. My sister and I spent hours lying on the warm linoleum floor that smelled like it had just come out of the factory. It gave us plenty of joy and warmth in our feet for quite a few years, until the political system changed and we were finally able to buy the elegant tiles, the kind my mother always wanted. Eventually, after Ala the housekeeper moved out, we took down the wall, opening up the kitchen and adding a huge window. The process took over thirteen years; I wish my dad had seen the finished room.

I remember my mom's kitchen as if it was a painting. Every morning before work, she'd set-up the table for me, always leaving me notes expressing her love. She was a big fan of colorful tablecloths and beautiful table settings, even if nothing matched. During spring and summer, the table displayed an array of fresh fruits in small baskets or strainers. Raspberries, blueberries, and cherries still with droplets of water were the centerpiece. On the wooden cutting board were the sliced tomatoes, cucumbers with a few pieces of "skin" to rub on our face and eyes, sour pickles and sauerkraut. The rest of breakfast constituted of fresh farmer's cheese mixed with sour cream and chives, some yellow cheese and fresh rolls with dark seeds. Fresh dill was set-up in a glass of water instead of flowers.

We loved farmer's markets and whenever we had a chance, we'd go together, getting up at five in the morning. The markets were crowded and beautiful. At the time, these were the only places that had an abundance of colorful foods from the nearby countryside. Some people came with horses and wagons. You had to bring your own jars to get the pickles and sauerkraut from the barrel, or the egg cartons in order to buy eggs. We had no plastic bags unless someone had a relative in a foreign country and sent a gift in one. You could spot people selling them on the streets and could even pick the design. We cherished those, especially the young people, as it was trendier to have one of these than the knitted ones. These reusable bags are making a comeback now, in this era of recycling. The knitted ones allowed others to see what was inside, and it wasn't uncommon to have a stranger ask about where you purchased something. We always tried to buy milk fresh from the cow, as the milk in the stores was often contaminated with traces of bluish detergent. The glass bottles used for the milk were reusable and washed; I supposed there were problems with the rinsing process. Nevertheless, it didn't kill us.

At home, there was always time to set-up the table and make hot cocoa, tea or coffee with milk before heading to school or work. My mom left for work at 7:30 am, she walked the main street and enjoyed the time on her own. I often ran back home with my friends during lunch break to have something to eat before classes resumed for the afternoon. I don't know how my mom did it, but there was always soup handy, made either first thing in the morning, or last thing the night before. Despite food shortages in Poland, we were never hungry; it seems as if we could eat a sandwich or an apple if we needed a snack. We ate dinner early, the meal usually consisted of soup and a second dish , like a piece of meat, legumes, and usually potatoes. The fast food of our day consisted of pieces of baguette topped with sliced mushrooms and cheese, waffles with fruit and whipped cream sold from small pick-up trucks, and the dairy places where you could stop by for a milkshake. This last one was my favorite, especially when it was located next to my high school. A lady with an apron and a head net ladled our choice of milk, half and half, or kefir from a metal bucket, then added spoonfuls of fruit preserves and mixed it in a blender. The only official "fast food" place was run by the government and called "Milk Bar." It had the most typical polish foods cooked right in the premises and available within minutes of ordering. It tasted delicious despite the unattractive plates and aluminum utensils. The chain is still around and still sponsored by the city. It is a wonderful place to eat a fulfilling meal for a small price. It is great for older people, students, anyone on a low budget, or those who wish to go back in time, as not much there has changed.

Whenever we had a chance during spring and summer, we went to flower markets and bought flowers as if we were florists. We put them in glass vases and filled our rooms with them, living every woman's fantasy to wake-up surrounded by flowers. We loved the warm months, the abundance of colors, and the variety of foods. We ate seasonally; fruits were not available during winter, so we only had root vegetables, frozen fruit, and pickles to get us by to the next season. When I was about seven years old, my mom went to New York for training. She brought me back a doll that opened and closed her eyes and said "Mama," as well as a big basket of Clementines. It was the best present ever. We felt rich because we had this exotic fruit filled with vitamin C in the middle of winter. At least for a while, I had a break from drinking beet juice to stay healthy. I despised the taste of it and always made a fuss, just like with Shark liver oil. My mom made a small hole inside the beet, filled it out with sugar and put it on the hot radiators to extract some juice. We defrosted strawberries the same way, waiting for hours until they became soft and juicy. Unlike the beets, they were delicious and we waited eagerly until they were ready.

My home was cozy and inviting, always full of visitors and food, even in the poorest times. But the conversations and the laughter that took place around the kitchen table were the most memorable part. When my mom got a bad case of giggles – which happened quite often and many times for no apparent reason – the whole table shook and everyone started laughing contagiously. My sister Kasia, born with Down Syndrome, had her own particular sense of humor. She stared grimly at us, eventually using a finger to draw a circle around her forehead, stating that we were all crazy.

Sometimes when the table shook too much, Kasia impatiently pushed herself away in one strong motion, shaking her head in disbelief and causing the liquids to spill. That never stopped us from laughing even harder. We often had friends or neighbors over and my mom could whip up a meal in no time. The cooking area was always a mess and the vegetables, pots and pans piled up quickly. Our sink was small, the drying rack even smaller and the faucet very thin; dishes were everywhere. On top of that, my mom tried to conserve energy by minimizing the amount of water used. Yet somehow, by the time I woke up the next day, the table was already set-up with a clean tablecloth and clean dishes. To me, it was a magical transformation.

After my father's death in 1979, only the three of us lived in the house, but it wasn't always like that. My paternal grandparents, who lost their home during the Second World War, moved into the house with my father. Soon after, my parents married and everyone lived together, they shared one room, divided only by a heavy curtain. They lived together for almost fifteen years, until the year I was born. My grandmother died in January of 1967 and my grandfather decided to follow her a month later. He died at the beginning of March and I was born at the end of the month. The joy of having a healthy daughter overtook the grieving. Then I suppose, for the first time, my parents felt free at home.

Times were tough; there were no easy options. Often, those who divorced ended-up living together, as there was no place else to go. The wealthy, prior to war, went from living in big apartments to living in communal housing with strangers. There was no other option, the new government made home owners turn their homes into communal residences, and they became no more than tenants, with the government having control of the house. Those houses had a common hallway, kitchen and bathroom.

My mom's father had to settle for communal living. After the war, he returned to his apartment. He received a promise from the government that he could stay there. My grandfather renovated the place only to find out he had to choose a tenant, or one would be assigned to him. No one back then had a say or influence in his or her own life. They had to adjust or lose their mind. And leaving the country wasn't easy. Nothing was easy at the time.

Sophie, my mom's best friend, lived in a house like that. It was old and beautiful. The entrance and staircase were made out of white marble, and the stair rails and tall heavy doors out of dark mahogany. The front door squeaked when pushed open revealing a different world, taking you back in time. You could still feel the old riches from the previous era staring at you in the form of beautiful chandeliers, ornamental door handles, and wooden floors with washed out designs. We never took our shoes off, but slid on old rags over to Sophie's room, I thought it was fun. She and her mother occupied two rooms. One was a long narrow room used as a living room, the other one was spacious and served as the bedroom. The old building had high ceilings; therefore, the rooms appeared bigger than they really were. The windows faced the square courtyard, and you could often see the inside of other people's rooms and definitely smell their cooking. The courtyard was at the center of the house and it had a prevalent echo, noises carried throughout the house from one end to the other. Everyone knew if a woman was wearing high heels simply by the traveling sound of her steps. Some people made it their pastime to lean over their windows and watch their neighbors. Sophie led a quiet life amongst the many interesting tenants. For example, one of them never showered and the smell of her body was detectable as one approached her floor. They all shared a kitchen and a tiny bathroom.

Sophie worked with my mom at the exporting company; she did personal Bible study, and was a lovely companion. Her hair was either orange or red. Back then, the only available hair dye was henna, but only in the reddish hues. It must have been frustrating for many women with dark hair to use the unflattering color to cover their gray. But one had to adjust, there was only one color available, and women like to cover their gray hair.

Sophie was a constant visitor in our home. She was part of us, sharing in joy and sadness. She was a devout Christian and old baccalaureate. That is until one day in her late forties, when she decided to marry Andrew, a character so obscure and strange we all decided she'd lost her mind. Sophie was soft-spoken, quiet and slow. The man she married looked like Rasputin; had long black hair and a thick mustache; he never showered, had no education and was an alcoholic. We all wondered what possessed poor old Sophie. Their marriage lasted for over ten years, and when Sophie was dying, he never left her side at the hospital. A few years later, he got into a dispute with his drinking companion, who stabbed him to death. Andrew was buried next to Sophie; a Rasputin and an Angel.

During her last visit at the hospital, my mom was able to thank Sophie for her friendship by saying simply: "Sophie, I love you!" I didn't get the chance to see her, but I would like to say: "Sophie, I loved you too!"

We didn't have any luxuries. Even though my grandfather was one of the first ones to have a car in the pre-war Warsaw, we never had one. We were lucky we had a telephone, since it often took years to get an assigned phone number. I still remember when a friend from school finally got a phone. I must have been one of the first callers. She answered by asking: "Who is it?", as if she was answering the door. That's when I first realized how awkward of a society we lived in.

People were on waiting lists even for automatic washers. Although automatic washers were available everywhere else, in Poland, and at our time, we still had manual washers. Some women worked as "washing ladies." They took your laundry home and brought it back cleaned and ironed. We never used one. Instead, Ala the housekeeper, along with my mom, boiled starch and submerge the sheets in it, making sure not to burn their hands. Sometimes they starched our pajamas, making us laugh at night, as we were barely able to move. They put all the whites in a tall aluminum pot filled with hot soapy water and boiled it for an hour to get the dirt out, turning it around with a wooden spoon like a pot of soup. They took all the laundry to the fifth floor attic to dry. It was an adventurous place for kids. It had tiny unsecured windows and a sandy floor, a stale smell and little light. The woman who managed the keys to the attic wasn't very pleasant or talkative, she often just extend her hand through a narrow door opening to give or take the keys from us. (I recently attended a Second World War reenactment, where women were showing the aluminum washboards, the ropes and the clips; the place where kids could put the wet rags through the small press with a handle to get the water out. I was watching my childhood from thirty some years ago in the middle of Europe).

We pressed sheets in a nearby laundry. For as long as I can remember, the same man worked in that place; he always wore a white tank shirt and smoked a cigarette. And it was always the same scene: he lifted the press, put in the clothes, he closed the press and held it down. Over and over. The sheets and tablecloths came back to us stiff and neatly folded. The same laundry place also changed the color of your clothes to the one you desired. It was a great idea, since clothes weren't widely available, we did everything to preserve or refresh what we already had. The fabric stores were pretty well stocked at the time, and we relied heavily on seamstresses. During my childhood, women wore skirts and stockings, but pantyhose were scarce as everything else, and women relied on repair services. No one could afford to throw away a pair simply because they had a run.

After the automated washer came the vacuum cleaner. I was afraid of it and jumped on the sofa in fear it might suck me in. My parents were able to purchase some other commodities. We replaced my grandmother's stove-heated curling iron with an electric one. Same with our old heavy iron, it even had an opening for a hot coal, a reminiscence of my grandparent's era. We washed the windows with soapy water and wiped them with newspapers sprayed with alcohol. We cleaned the wooden floors with water, waxed them on our knees, and polished them by the whole family dancing on rags. Our napkins were transparent, and toilet paper resembled sand paper. We didn't complain though, and considered ourselves lucky if we were able to buy it. Sometimes we stood in line a few times if the store imposed quotas on rolls per person. My mom, my sister and I, often pretended we didn't know each other just to get more in one shot.

Our lives in the late 70's and early 80's revolved around getting food, clothes, and everyday staples. The majority of those things required stamps. Stamps allowed you to buy a few pounds of meat, a few bars of soap, and a bottle or two of alcohol per month. Those who didn't drink, swapped for the meat stamps. However, having the stamps did not guarantee you would get the products. You still had to search the stores and stand in line. Many times lines formed days in advance just in case there would be meat available. Nobody knew what kind of meat would be available, they just knew a delivery was coming soon. People waited for days and nights, forming friendships or enemies that would either allow them to leave the line to get some rest and eat, or to be afraid to leave the line. My mom never stood in line. We tried to be in good spirits, and whenever we thought we had it bad, we joked about waiting in lines to get the wrong pair of shoes, and hoping to swap them in the black market for the right item. Salaries were the same across the board, with slight differences among certain professions and definitely differed between men and women. We lived from month to month and without luxuries. Vacations at the resorts were organized through workplaces at inexpensive rates and summer camps were subsidized by them so that parents didn't have to worry about the kids.

At some point, my mother considered moving to Sweden, but she brought us back home. We were never hungry, never lonely. We mattered in our community to our friends and family. My mom didn't want to lose that. We certainly had some regrets, especially when I was thirteen years old and military tanks appeared on our street and no one knew whether they were Russian or Polish, but years later, we knew we made the right decision. Despite all the shortages and difficulties of daily living, we were always happy. Our home was like our castle and that's all that mattered to us. We felt safe and we had a strong sense of belonging.

December 13th of 1981 began as usual. It must have been a

weekend, as I remember my mother cooking in the kitchen during the day. I tried to turn on the TV, but all I got was a flat intermission signal. I tried to call my friend, but the phone was dead. Soon after, my girlfriend came and announced there were tanks on the streets. We didn't know if we were at war against the Soviets or if they had invaded our country. We were scared. Later on, we learned that members of the pro-democracy Solidarity were imprisoned, people vanished out of their homes, and Lech Walesa – the leader of the Solidarity movement – was detained. All communication was cut; the phone lines disconnected (to add to the confusion), school was out and TV brought us only General Jaruzelski's speeches. Armed vehicles patrolled the streets, we had a curfew, and they enforced a six-day working week.

It was hard to adjust to 6 days of schooling and work. Even though the extra day was shorter than the rest, it left us with barely any time to relax and to be together. All the parties had to end early because of curfew, and parents usually walked into the room with an alarm clock sending us home on time. We were too young to be part of the opposition, but were aware of what was going on. We wore small electronic resistors attached to the watch bracelets as safe demonstrators of our political views. My mom, who was a member of the Solidarity movement, was warned at work to stop her association with it or lose her job. She kept her involvement private, as she was the only breadwinner for her two daughters, but she never signed-out. I participated in demonstrations with my mom whenever they were close to the house. We lived off the main street of Warsaw and could run home fast whenever the tearing gases were thrown into the crowds.

The Soviets didn't invade us, but the threat continued. We had to live, hoping our voices reached other corners of the world. To suit political propaganda, they rewrote our history books, but we learned the real facts from our parents and family. In fifth grade, Russian became a mandatory subject and they taught it in school. We despised it, doing everything we could to pass without learning it. Years later, I learned Russian from my children's Ukrainian nannies. They are the ones that made the language beautiful and worth learning.

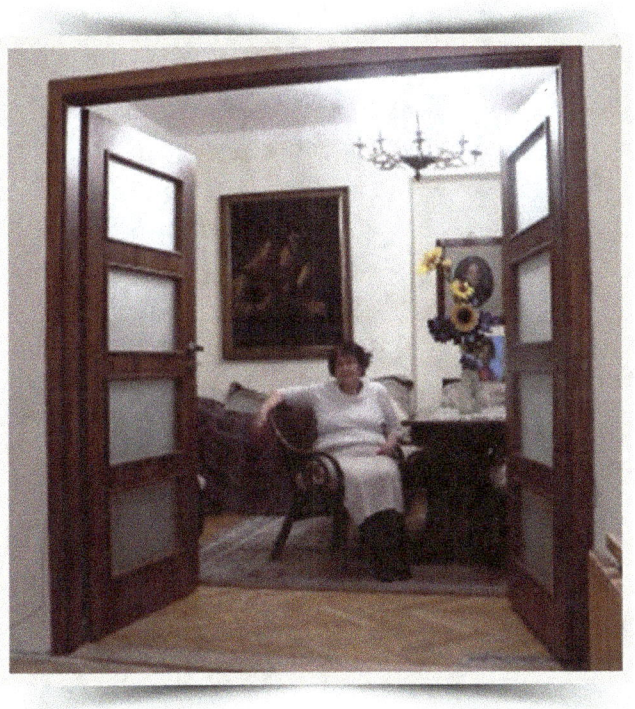

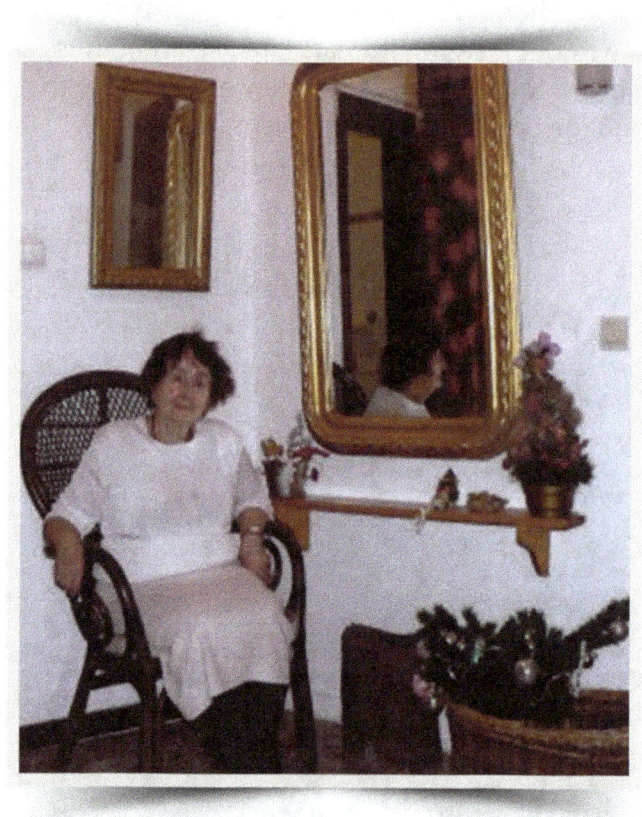

Mom at home, 2011

"A different way of perceiving"

Life of an artist with Down Syndrome
Kasia Puciata 1961-2004

It is not the length of life, but the depth of life.
Ralph Waldo Emerson

My big sister Kasia was born with Down Syndrome in 1961, in Warsaw, Poland, in a culture not well prepared to welcome people with any kind of disabilities. Although, 16 years after the end of the Second World War, one could imagine there were disabled people in Poland. Anything that did not seem "normal" was immediately unwanted and openly referenced using derogatory language with sarcastic undertones. Quite often, my mom tried to shift people's perceptions by explaining quietly that her daughter was ill. Still, even while Down syndrome was considered an illness back then, it didn't justify certain behaviors, like saying something odd, burping out loud, or laughing uncontrollably. For many, those behaviors were unacceptable. People rejected her simply for her looks, since they did not fit our social standards of beauty and "normal."

When Kasia was little, she was cute and huggable. As she grew older, and especially after our father passed away and she started taking medication for her mental-health, she withdrew

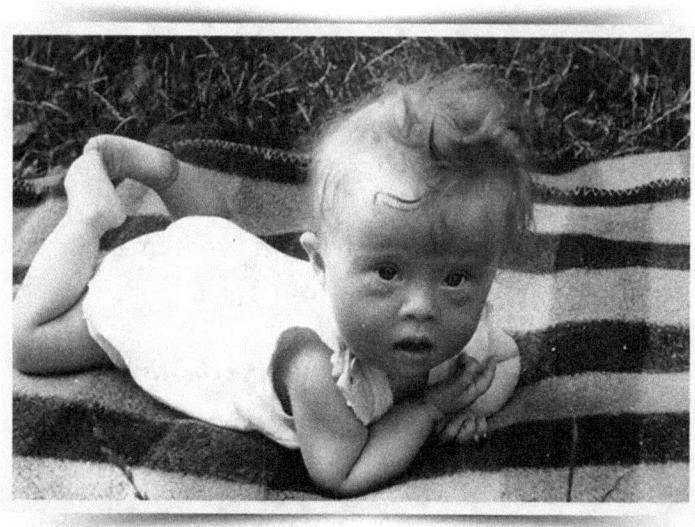

into her own world and the physical characteristics of Down syndrome seemed more pronounced. The medication made her gain weight, especially in the hips, making the rest of her body seem disproportionally smaller. She was just Kasia to us, but many people were ashamed of her, even close family members. Some requested that Kasia stay at home when we were invited over for dinner; others advised putting her in a mental institution or foster home, as to not ruin our family's good image. That was the advice my mom got from her own mother, while my father's mother wouldn't even look at the newborn for a month. I can't even imagine how hard it was on my mom, who saw an absolute beauty in her child from the very first moment she was born. I was brought up knowing that if Kasia was born normal, she would have been a rare beauty, like Snow White, with ebony hair, an alabaster complexion, and a gentle demeanor. Mom would often point out her tiny ears, her well-defined eyebrows, and her perfectly shaped nose. She knew every inch of Kasia's body, caressing it with words of admiration and love. My nanny was a simple girl from the countryside, so Kasia had an old-fashioned governess, an older widowed lady who was there not only to take care of her, but to teach her manners and whisper patriotic poetry into those tiny ears. There were many good people in our lives, but there were also many who didn't have compassion for her.

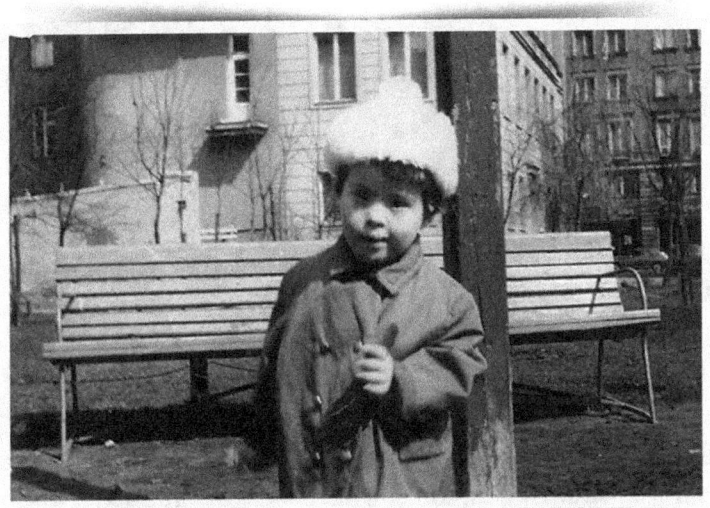

My paternal grandfather showed a lot of affection for Kasia. I never knew him, as he passed away a couple of weeks before I was born in March of 1967, but I remember seeing a silver coin in a beautiful silver sack that he gave to my sister. It hid among all the jewelry. It was a cherished symbol of love, a valuable token that demonstrated that she was worthy of such a treasure in the eyes of her grandfather.

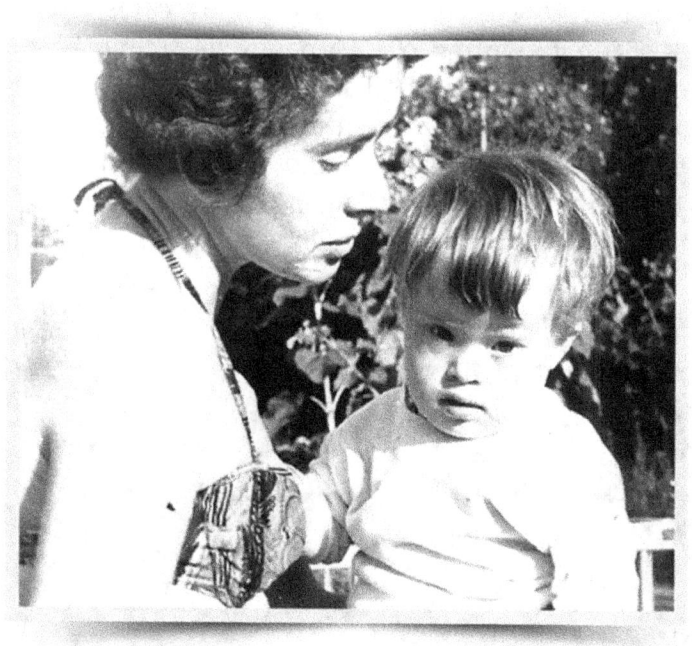

Mom and Kasia, always together

People, especially children, paused and stared at her, as if she was a member of a circus show. It was rough and painful for my sister, who would come home and look at herself in the mirror asking why she was different and if she was beautiful. We always laughed and said she was too beautiful for others to handle. She reached out for Nivea cream and smudged it over her face to ensure that beauty.

Many times my mom and I fought the cultural vulgarity, scaring the spectators away, making them ashamed for a split second. Children and young men were the cruelest, being highly entertained by what they saw and many times offensive. When Kasia was maybe five years old, a group of boys from a small countryside village where my parents were vacationing took great pleasure in teaching Kasia how to swear. She took a deep interest in those words, swearing like a peasant for the next decade! These vulgarities stuck, sending a shockwave through people who didn't know Kasia. It hurt us deeply, but we laughed our way through it. Twenty years after Kasia stopped swearing, she still obsessed over it. She often asked, "Joanna, do I swear?" and shake her head, murmuring a bad word quietly under her breath, in which case I'd say: "No, Kasia, it is me who swears!" and I would let the wave of bed words come out of my mouth. It was a game for us. We either had to protect Kasia from others or from herself, turn it around into a joke and laugh about it. This is how I approached things with my friends, smoothly transitioning their reactions from discomfort to acceptance to sincere laughter. It was much easier to train a young mind than to overcome adult perceptions.

In a radio interview given around 1990, my mom said bitterly that a dog was treated with more compassion than my sister was, because not only was my mom alone with her feelings, she was also rejected. Back then, there were no organizations that helped families cope or provide support and answers. There were mental institutions, there were Catholic nuns that provided extended care, but there were no support groups. My parents were strong on their own. While my father was alive and walking, people respected us much more. He was tall, handsome, and possessed class, which automatically created respect. My mom was beautiful and fragile, and when left alone she was much more vulnerable. She had to toughen-up and she called herself a Soviet tank. There was no room for depression in it, she was determined to feed us and raise us. When dad passed away, she vowed to herself we would never go hungry. I pictured this as similar to the scene from Gone with the Wind, where Scarlett O'Hara stood on top of the hill with a tightened fist vowing the same.

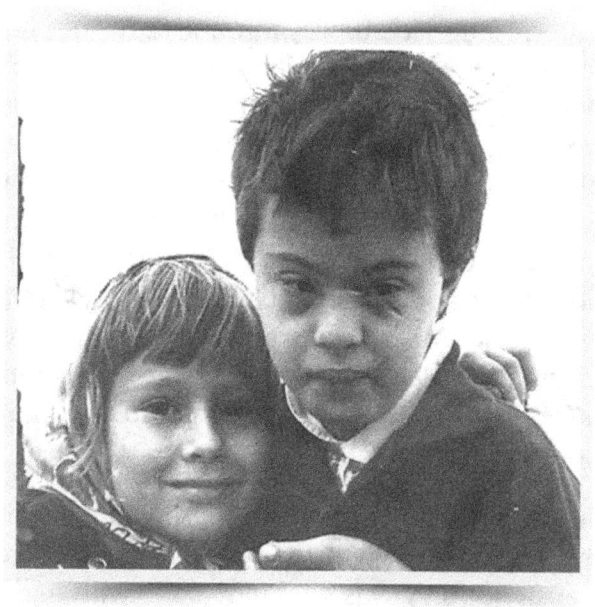

Kasia and I at the Baltic Sea

I quickly picked-up my mom's defensive attitude and when I felt brave I declared, "What are you staring at? Look at yourself! Do you think you are any better?" Sometimes we simply put our arms protectively around Kasia and pretend there was nobody around us. The later became a norm, as over the years, people around us got used to Kasia's presence, allowing for friendships to be formed. The whole street knew who she was. She made rounds from store to store, just hanging around. The grocery store or meat store, where she had a cup of coffee and her favorite Veal Vienner. Or the barber shop, where she helped out by holding pins during perms and sitting next to the cash register sipping another cup of black coffee.

From early on she seemed to search for life's purpose. She didn't like to be idle and participated in as many activities as she could, taking advantage of the small freedoms of independence. Before our father passed away, Kasia went out on her own to make her "rounds," or to simply relax at the playground. She had the keys to the house, she was able to board the bus independently and ride to her school without us. She walked back home, making stops at her favorite stores, where over the years she became everybody's friend and was welcomed everywhere.

Kasia and Dad were incredibly close. He was her only companion when mom was at work and I was at school. During the last years of his illness, she was the one serving him breakfast, preparing his tea, and making sure he had what he needed. She knew what to do when his legs shook uncontrollably; she pressed on them gently until they stopped. She opened the doors for the nurses, answered phones, and went to the bakery to pick-up some bread, or to the kiosk to buy his cigarettes. She knew how to prepare Turkish coffee and drank it with Dad in a ceremonial way, serving it in nice porcelain cups. She knew how to warm up lunch. She could even make noodles, her favorite dish. In their spare time, Kasia and Dad listened to the radio while Kasia copied the alphabet from the ABC book. She never mastered it fully, but she enjoyed the practice. It was much harder for her to write than paint. But she was a workaholic and she practiced her alphabet daily for hours. Kasia and Dad were always together, it came to no surprise how hard it was for her to deal with his loss.

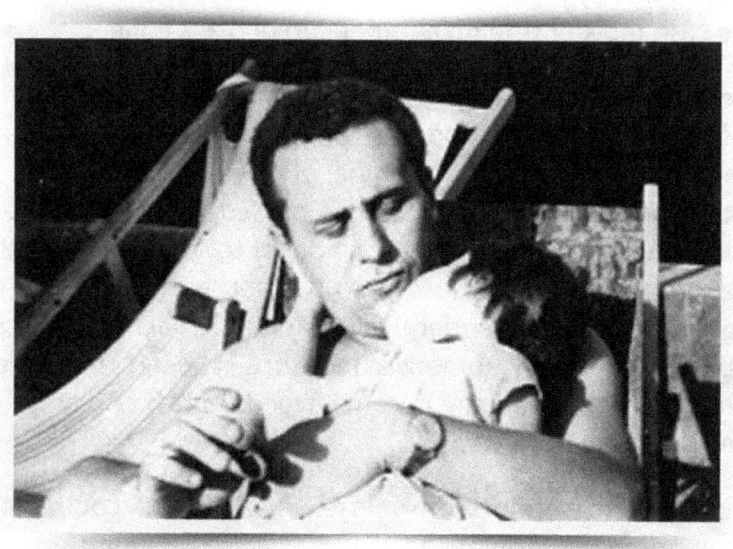

Kasia and Dad

Kasia was a careless, giggling person, having a sense of belonging. That Kasia was gone when tragedy struck and changed her life forever. Our father, Kasia's best friend, passed away unexpectedly. The nightly ambulances that took him to the hospital were nothing new at our house, but he always came back. On September 15, 1979, when I was only twelve and Kasia was eighteen years old, he didn't. Kasia and I cleaned his room, changed the bed sheets, rearranged the furniture and waited quietly for our mom's return. I remember getting sweets from the cafe and feeling very proud to be able to help. Our mom came home quiet but with an unknown presence. She told us dad passed away, a concept I did not fully comprehend. Kasia, on the other hand, started laughing and giggling as if something funny took place. Before the funeral, she announced that dad came to her all dressed-up in a black suit. We got scared.

The day after the funeral, I woke in the middle of the night due to Kasia bursting into my room laughing uncontrollably, mom right behind her trying to calm her down. That was the last time we heard her clear voice for a long two-year period of relative silence. She took the loss of her best friend and daily companion hard. She retreated into her inner world and shut down. She claimed to see ghosts, had conversations with God, Dad, and scary creatures who come after her. She pursed her lips and shook her head when we asked her questions. She responded with a barely audible whisper, "I am not talking!" Sometimes, mom got frustrated and yelled at her asking to tell her about the things she saw, and then both of them ended frustrated.

We tried to turn things around the only way we knew how, through laughter. That definitely helped us. We whispered at the table, pretending we were the ones seeing a ghost or my dad coming out of the corner. Kasia's reaction could go two ways: she either got-up abruptly or looked at us as if we were completely crazy and lost our sanity. Usually she followed it by telling us to "knock on our forehead", meaning, make sure there is some brain in there. That usually brought us the moments we waited for, where we all began to giggle. Maybe we didn't just do it for Kasia, maybe it was a way out for all of us, a way to cope with what seemed like a highly depressive situation.

Kasia seemed to have a keen awareness of the spiritual world, although we often wondered if this was not a result of her heavy medications. She claimed God and Archangel Gabriel showed up to visit her, but she also saw demons (ghosts, as she called them) and she was quite scared of them. That is when she seemed to stare into space with eyes wide open, and the reason we began laughing and "seeing" ghosts too. While Kasia's visions seemed dark, she always searched for God. When the priest refused to give her Communion, she snuck in front of the line during Sunday Mass and got it anyway. She was determined to go to Heaven and spend eternity with God, hence, many of her painting reflected that, along with her understanding of how He judges people and what Heaven is really like. She claimed she was the only one who knew such mysteries.

" There are small rooms in Heaven, beds, two rooms and two beds. Who lives there? All that feel safe about the future. She announces that not all will fit, and she will have to drop out of school."Kasia

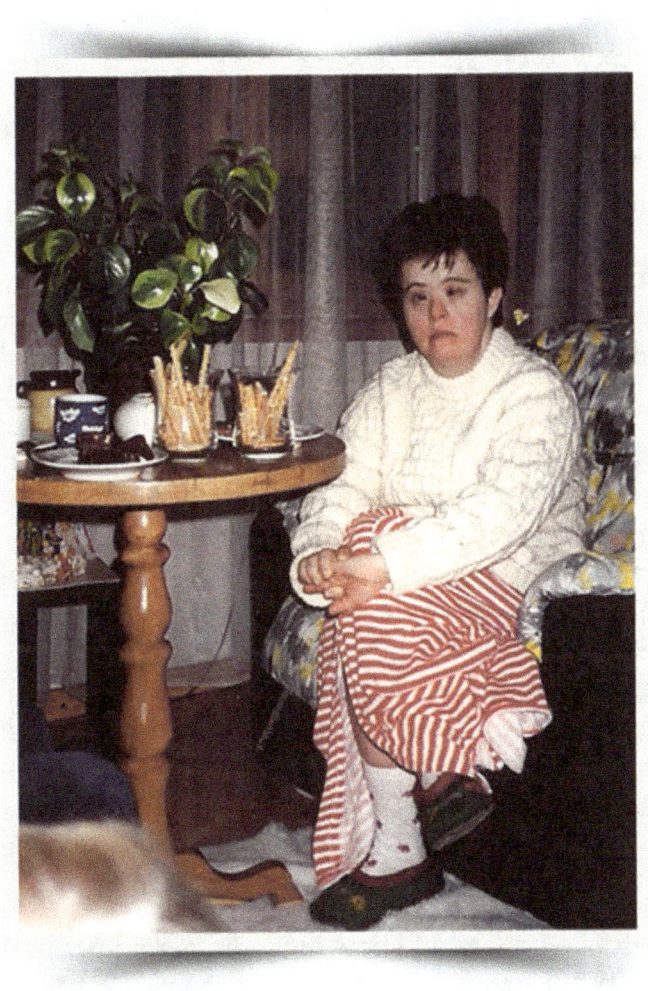

Sleepover at my girlfriend's

Yes, my mom worried and did everything she could to help, to protect, and to medicate, but by creating laughter, we survived and continued to make a home people wanted to visit. My friends were not afraid to come over. My first boyfriend, who later became my husband, was not afraid to fall in love with someone whose sister would forever be a part of our lives. Mom paved the way for all to accept Kasia through her own attitude of acceptance and unconditional love. None of my friends ever said that. "Joanna has an abnormal sister." Instead they said she was ill, which was the understanding of Down syndrome at the time. Mom rarely used that word, instead she called Kasia "different". As my friend Ola, who is a great a fashion designer and artist says, "The only difference is Beauty"

It did take heavy medication and hospitalization for Kasia to talk again, but it was never the same afterwards. She turned to music to liven-up the room and quiet down her thoughts. She became inseparable from her tape player and radio; silence became unbearable. On the other hand, music from dawn to night became too much for us and I remember pleading with Kasia to turn the radio down. Sometimes she would, yet sometimes she would crank it all the way up causing everybody to jump in their seats. She enjoyed that. Sometimes she laughed at us and ran to the other room, and sometimes she seriously announced she would not smile if she could not listen to her music. Even when she whispered under her breath, we could understand what she was saying.

I never quite understood how my mom picked-up on Kasia's desires, but she somehow knew what she needed. The radio, the knitting and embroidery, the guitar. Kasia loved to dance and hit the guitar strings with her fingers creating chaotic sounds that made sense only to her. She took the guitar with her frequently and sat down with it at the playground when she could still go out by herself. I often see myself in her, constantly searching for my own hidden talents, asking conscious questions about who I am. Kasia had to work through her subconsciousness to satisfy the hunger for knowledge. She was always like this. Years of practicing writing from the elementary book of ABC's, years of dedicated guitar playing, years of knitting and embroidering, and finally years of painting. Each passion lasted for years and gave her a purpose to wake-up.

In 1986 I finished high school and didn't pass the entry exam to the University of Warsaw. I thought about going to France to study abroad, as the borders were slowly beginning to open up. It wasn't a problem anymore to obtain a visa to Western Europe, but it was difficult to travel to the US. It happened that my high school sweetheart received a scholarship to the Western Michigan University through his father, a political refugee, who tough at this school. I somehow obtained a one-month visa to visit him, but when the time came to come back, we made a completely wild decision for me to stay. The only thing I remember asking myself was who was going to take care of Kasia in case something happened to mom. But I was very young and thought to myself, "I'll worry about it tomorrow".

My conversation with my mom went something like this: "Mom, we won't be seeing each other for a while". That was all I could say in a five-minute, expensive telephone conversation. Mom could not ask any questions, I only heard a silent "Ah!" coming out of her heart. The phones were still tapped, a leftover from the 1980 martial law. The Solidarity movement was active and strong and changes were coming, but in 1986 I was still coming from behind the "iron curtain". If I said anything else during that conversation, mom could be in trouble. The Polish Secret Service, called UB, was ever present and knew everything that went on in people's lives. Soon the word got out at mom's work that Joanna wasn't coming back from America. They questioned mom and she wasn't allowed to travel on business trips for a while. Since she was one of the best sales representatives the company ever had, they soon lifted the restriction, as working for an exporting company without the ability to travel to clients was simply impossible.

While mom's position was threatened because of my decision to immigrate to America, I was carelessly planning my future. Kasia's world became shattered once again; another person disappeared from her world. She asked about me every day, she asked if was coming back, but she knew I wasn't, she just knew. For a number of years, mom noted Kasia's thoughts in a special journal. Here is one of the entries:

"My house became very silent, less people come to visit ever since my second daughter left. Kasia respected her a lot. Joanna loved Kasia but did not tolerate her deviant behavior. Kasia never even thought to misbehave next to her. Now when Joanna asks questions in her letters, "Is Kasia practicing her writing? Is she smiling?" Kasia does that right away. Kasia knew that Joanna loved her very much and that she will be with her all her life."

It was now 1989. Ten years since dad's passing and three years since my leaving. Kasia was 28 years old. She turned from being a happy and outgoing child, to someone who had to search within her inner world to shine some light onto the real one. That's when she picked-up a pen and stared drawing meticulously and without breaks. Small circles, letter like artistic expressions, a cemetery with crosses. It had to make sense to mom since she bought her paints and white paper. Through her loving eyes, she saw something brilliant. Mom created a working space for Kasia and started showing her artwork to all the guests coming through our house. A breakthrough came when a well know art critic, Andrzej Oseka, a frequent guest of our upstairs neighbor, Ms. Wanda, saw some of the earlier paintings.

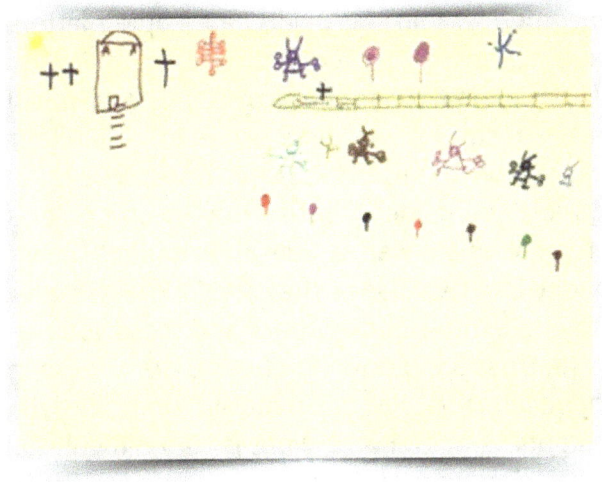

One of the earliest drawings

He declared my sister had a talent. Here is what he had to say about Kasia's art in the June 19th, 1992 article published in the Gazeta Wyborcza:

"In one of the naves of the church of the Savior (kosciol Zbawiciela) in Warsaw, you can see a small exhibition of gouache sketches, compositions almost abstract, amongst which we find the simplest sign-like motives depicting a tree, a window or a road. Sometimes we look up into a high bright space in which, in accordance with the intentions of the artist, we recognize the interior of the church.

Bold, strongly and confidently constructed paintings resemble the "informal" style of the early 1960's, particularly Soulage's. A little like de Staël. However all aesthetic influences are impossible here. The author, Kasia Puciata, was born with Down's Syndrome. The usual way of perceiving was not available to her. She tried – with the help of those close to her – to somehow join the world. She copied letters from a first grade schoolbook, tried embroidery and playing the guitar. Three years ago she tried painting for the first time. I consider the results astounding. It has to be a different way of perceiving since this art is so mature, so beautiful. The paintings are maintained consistently in one color scheme. Usually the colors are warm, juicy and soaring. The world has been divided into two planes; the first, dark, with muted colors, opens up into a more distant space and there you see nature, air, sun. The trees are blooming and the grass is green. Bright hues connect artistically with muted ones. Together they form perceptible matter and, what is very difficult to achieve in a flat painting, spatial depth. Unexpectedly landscapes of the romantics aren't brought to mind. This is emotional art, romantic, and the style of execution remains always similar. Through a dark frame you see a bright and colorful world."

Kasia passed away on Feb 16, 2004. She knew she was going. My last conversation with her was February 7, 2004.

Mom's Notes: – I put the cell phone in Kasia's ear. Joasia was crying. When she asked "Do you love me?" Kasia nodded her head to say yes.

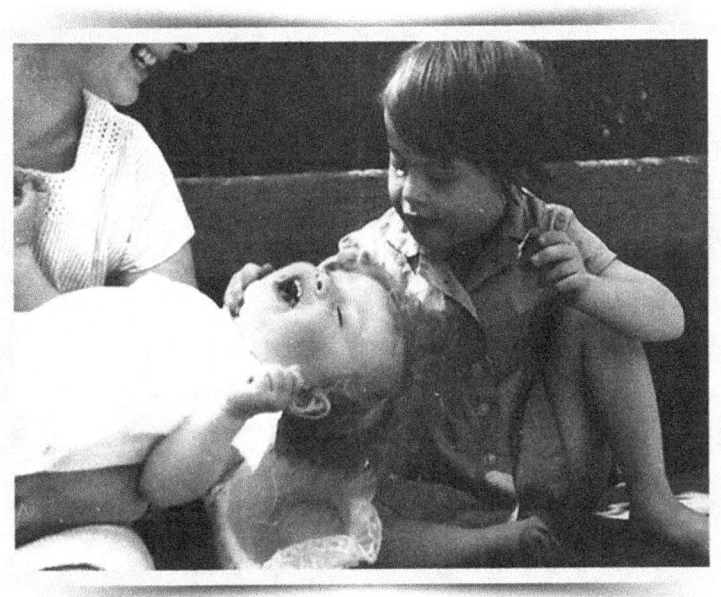

Mom, Kasia and I, 1967

❧ Journal thoughts ☙

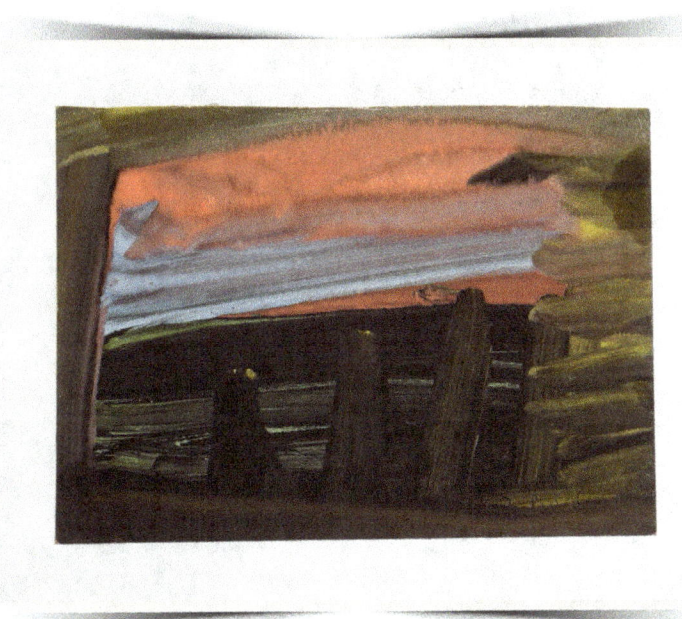

My legs rusted.

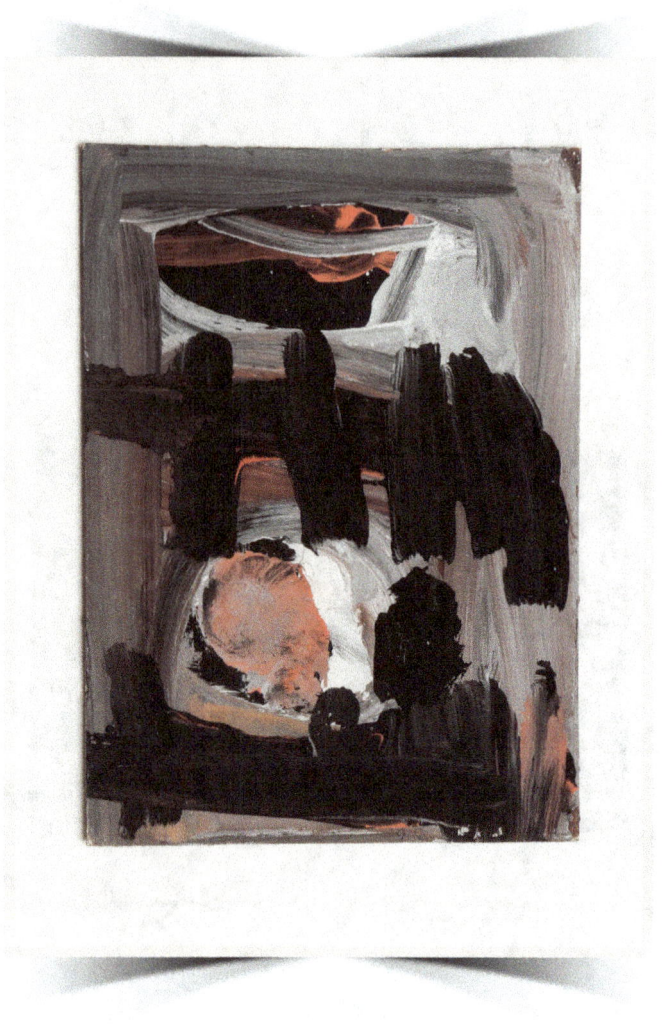

Where do you dream?

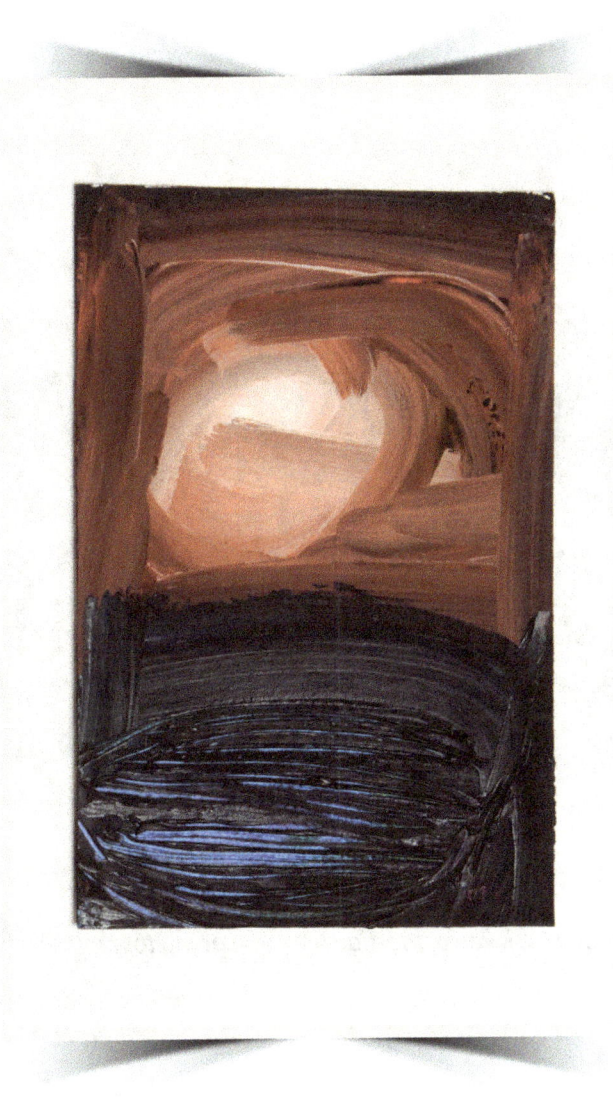

What is Heaven like?

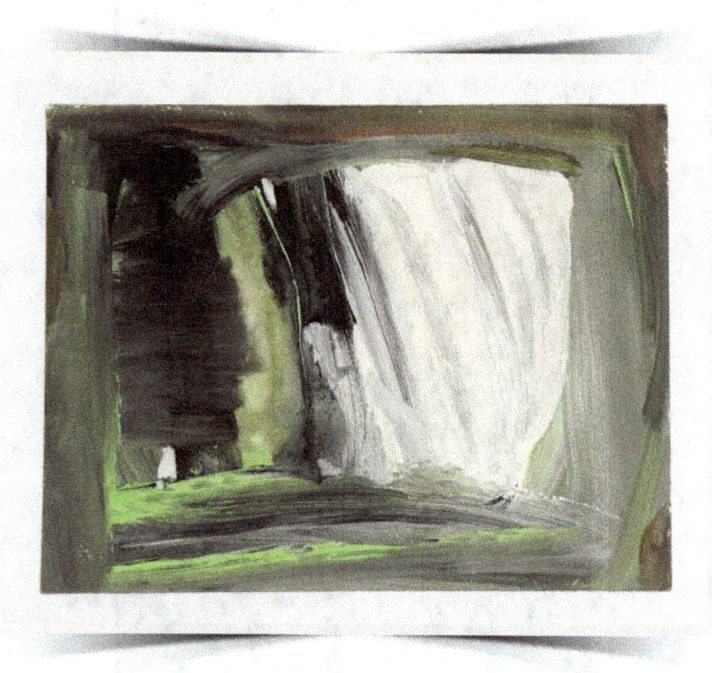

Can I ask you a question? Are you going to hurt me?

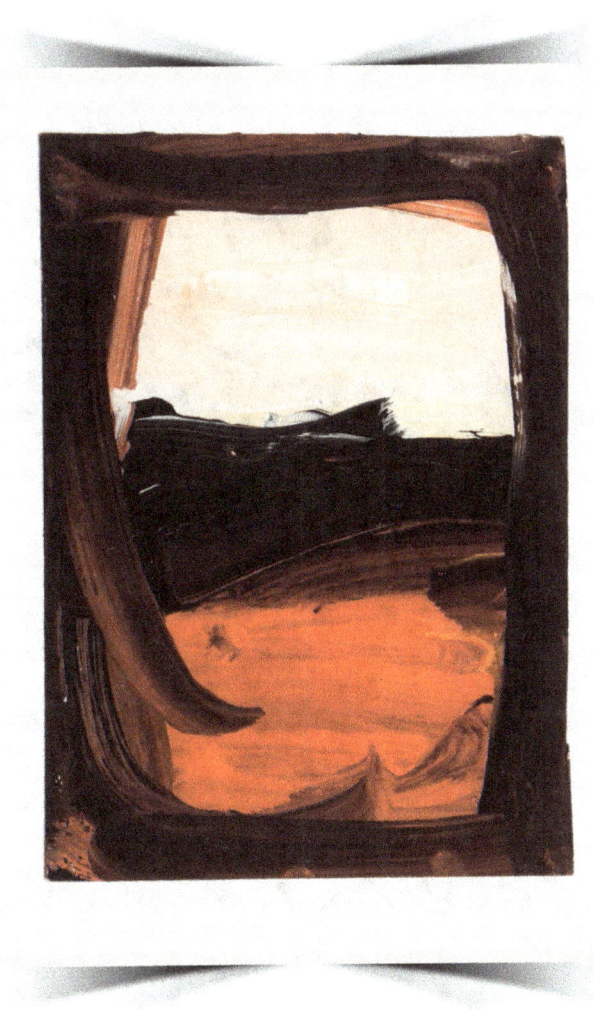

I wish to be as I was before, to look different, to look like Kasia.

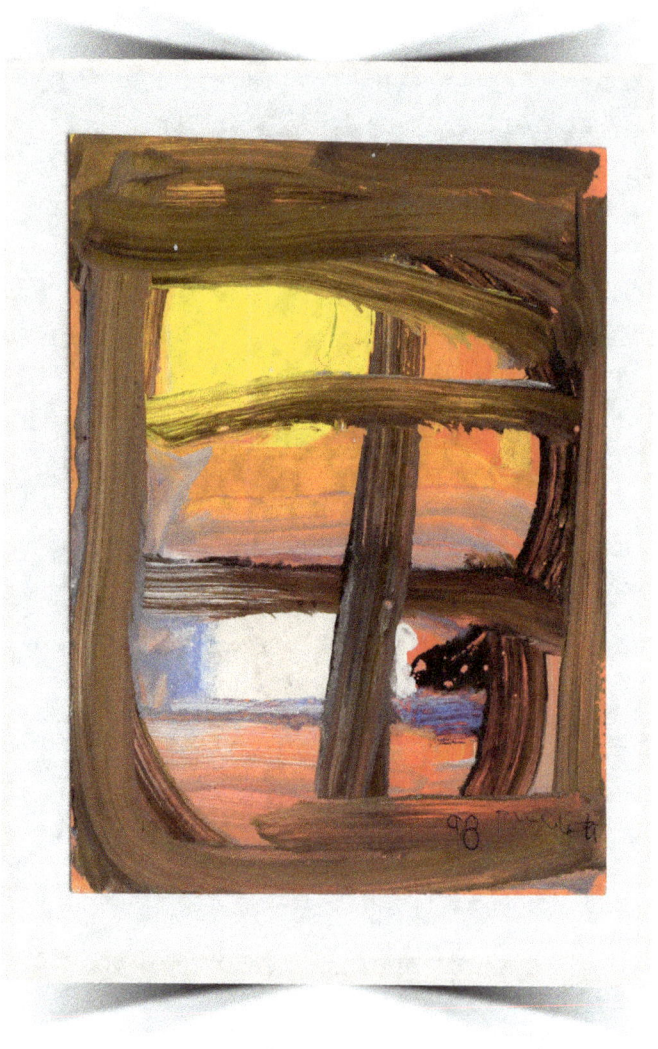

Spring is coming.

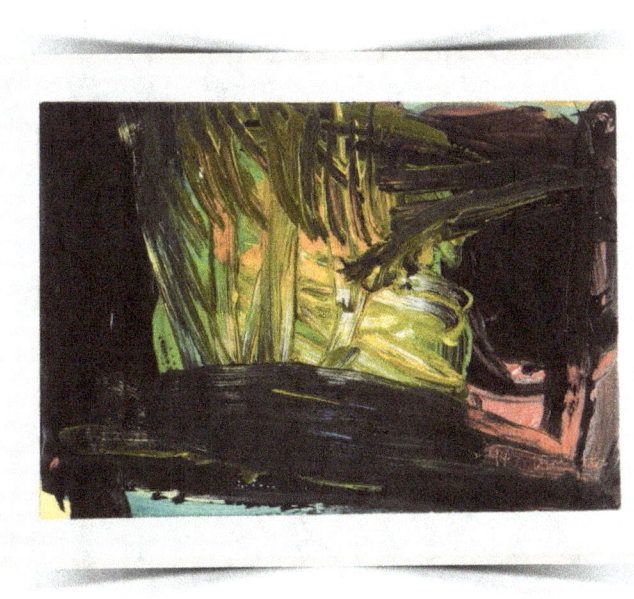

I feel good today and that tomorrow I will be normal

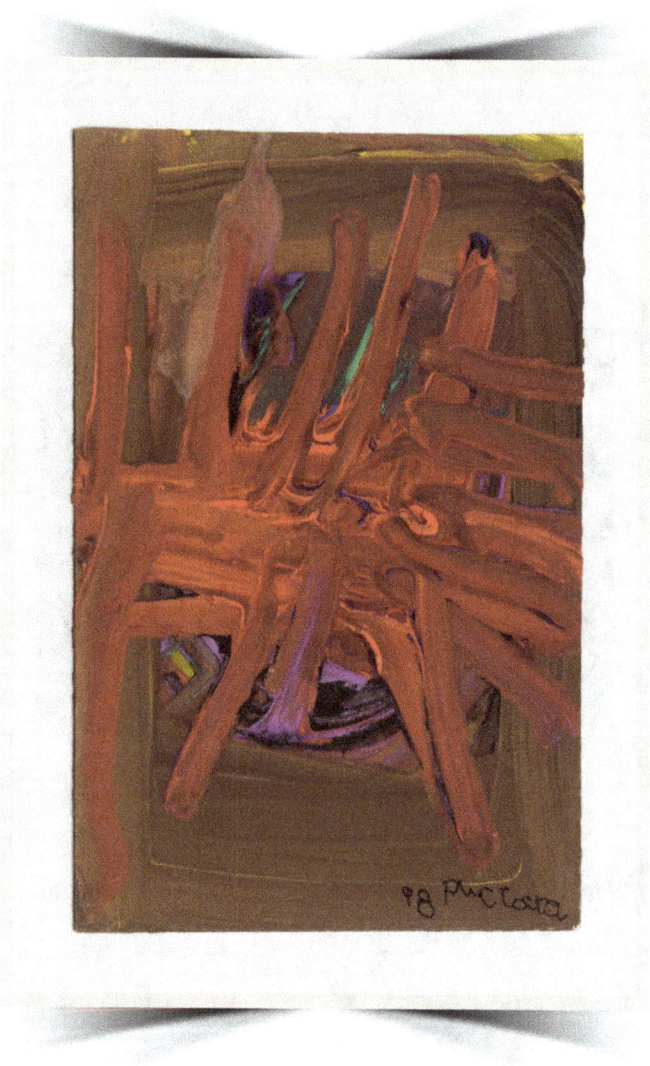

The doctor checked if I was normal.

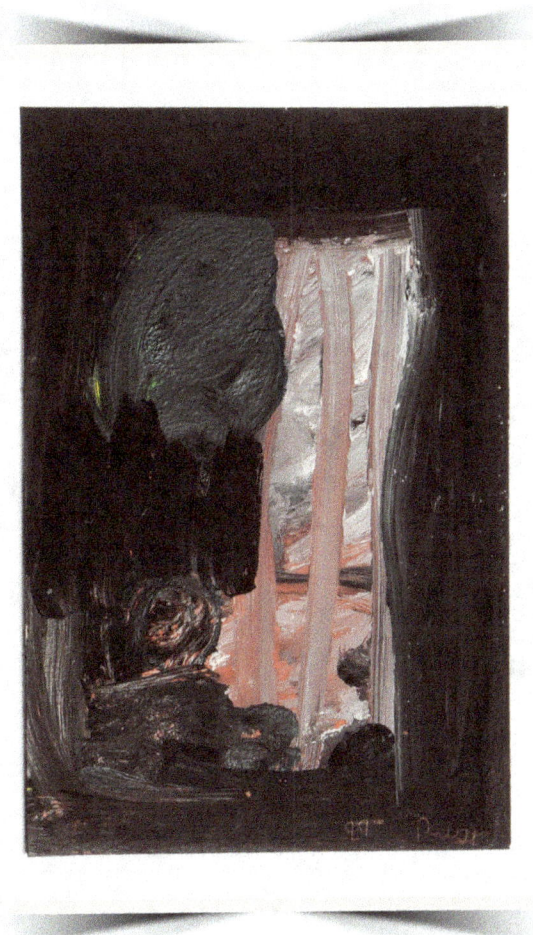

Why are you staring at the computer screen,
and not looking at me?

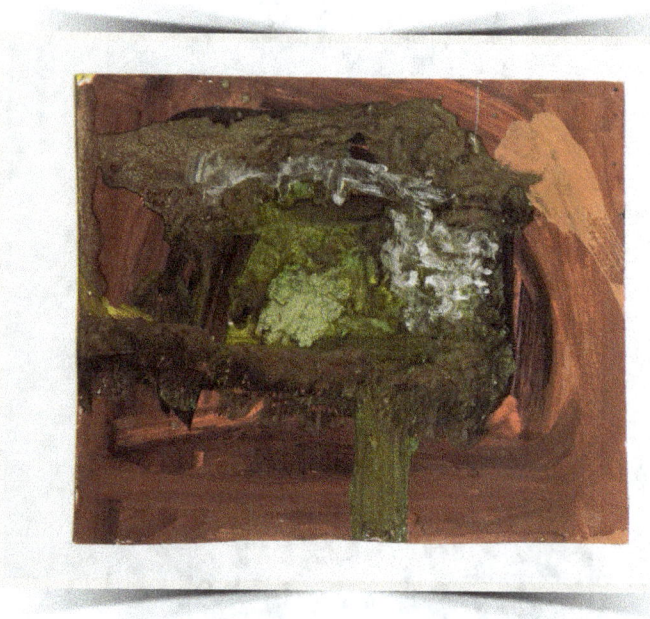

I wonder about tomorrow, will mom talk to me?
She's looking, but can't see me!

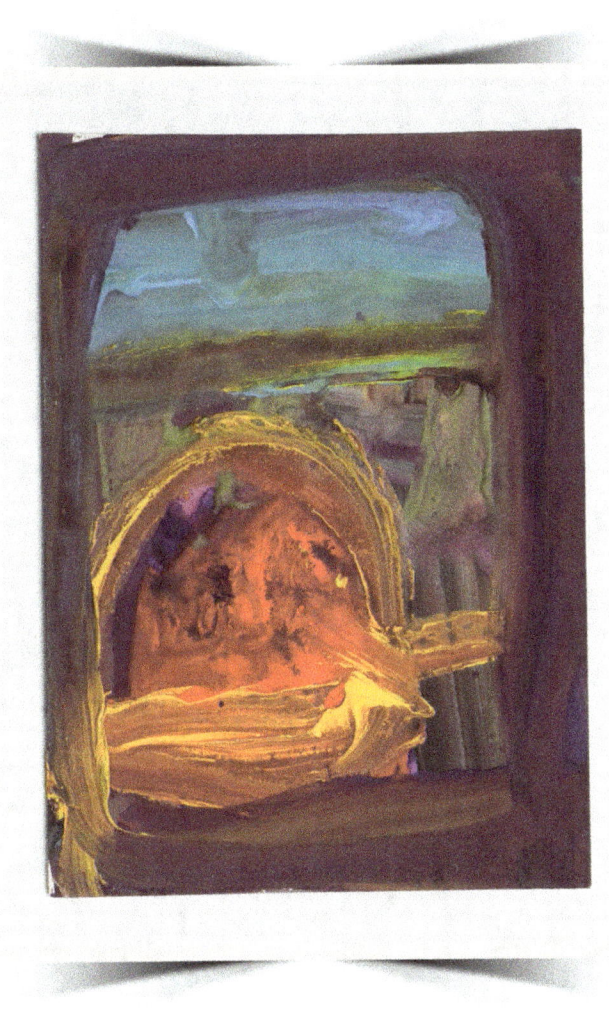

I have no ambition to go to school!

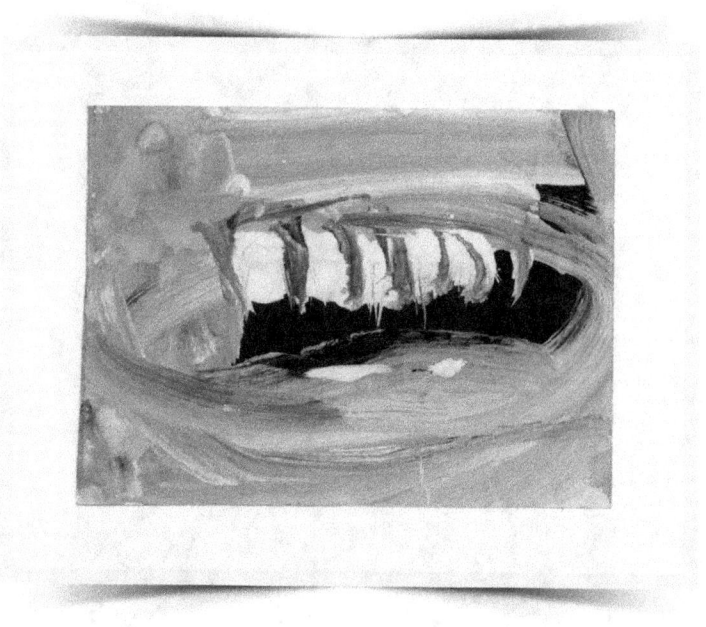

There is nothing to eat – and that's most important!

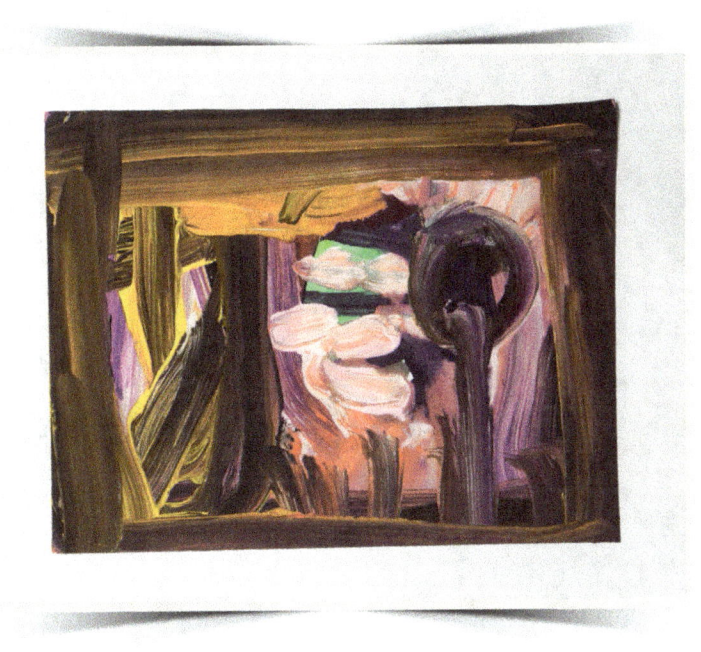

Breakfast was luxurious.

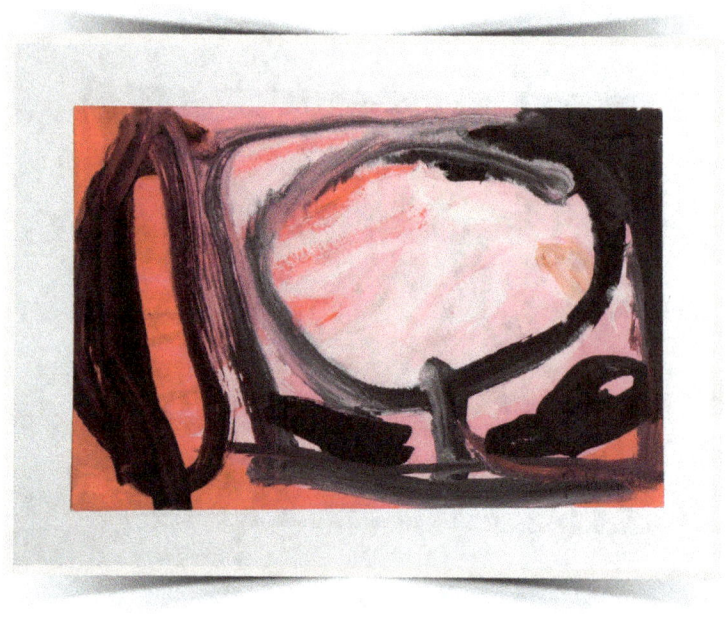

I want my paintings to be full of expression.

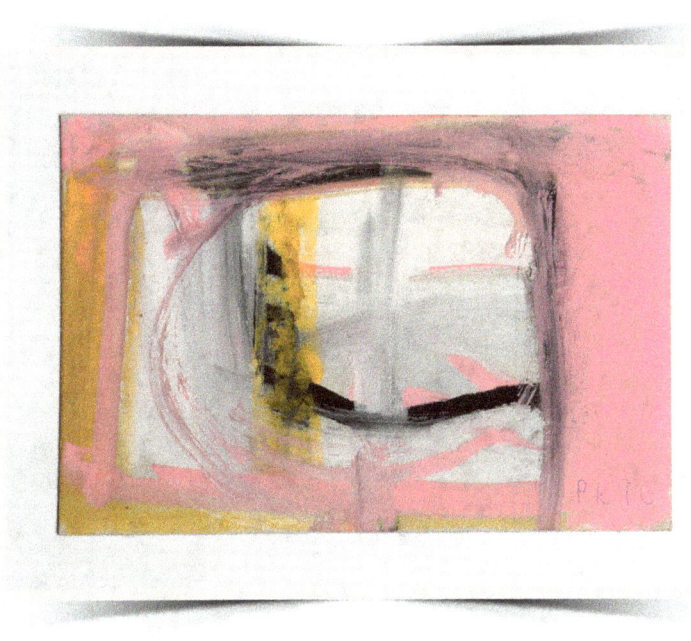

I like you lately.

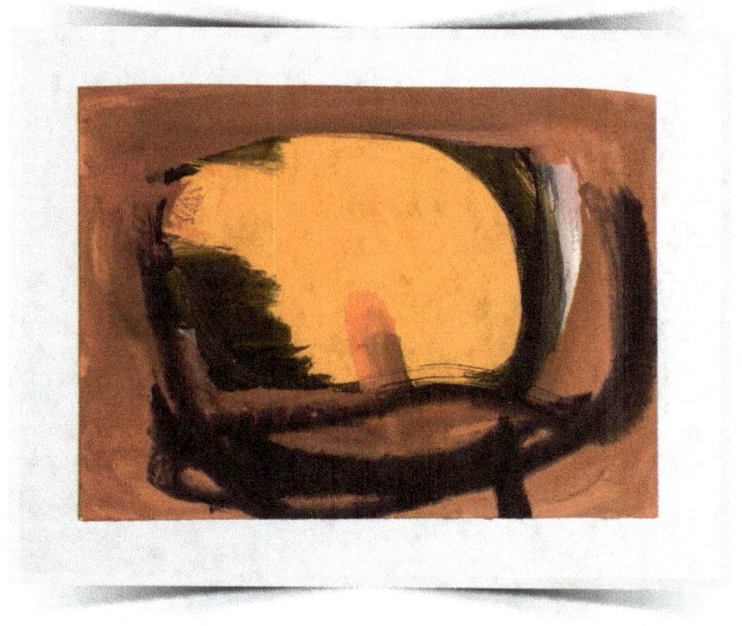

Mommy doesn't know I exist!

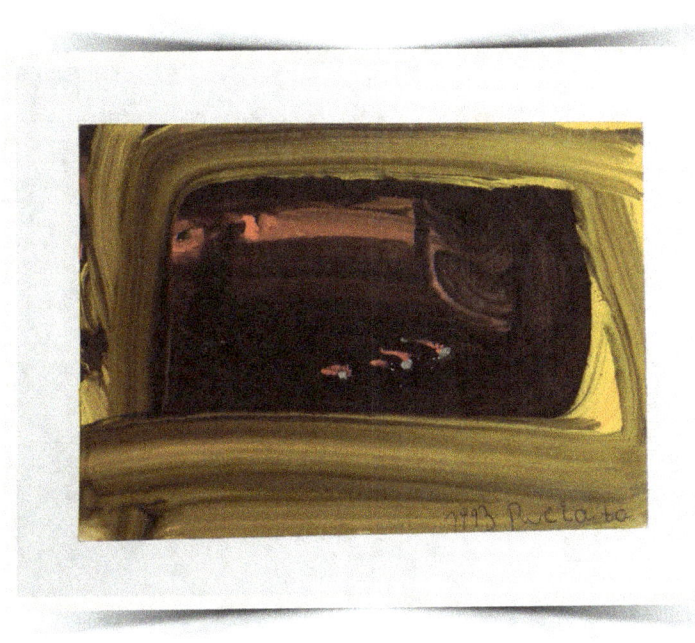

Mom, I pray for you.

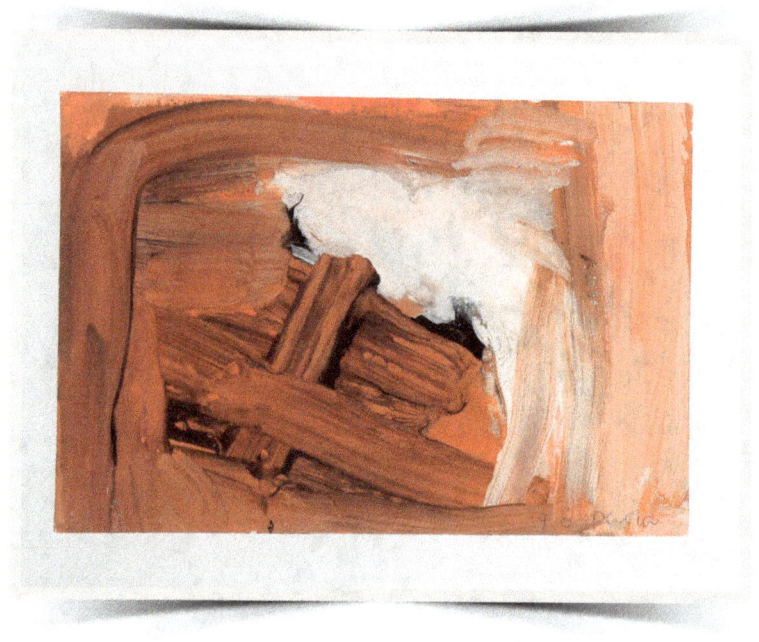

Today I feel good.

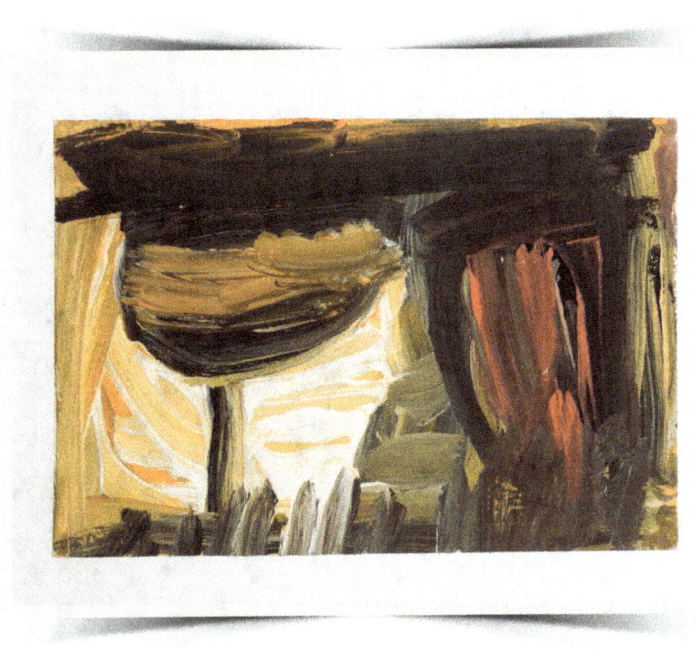

I am lonely.

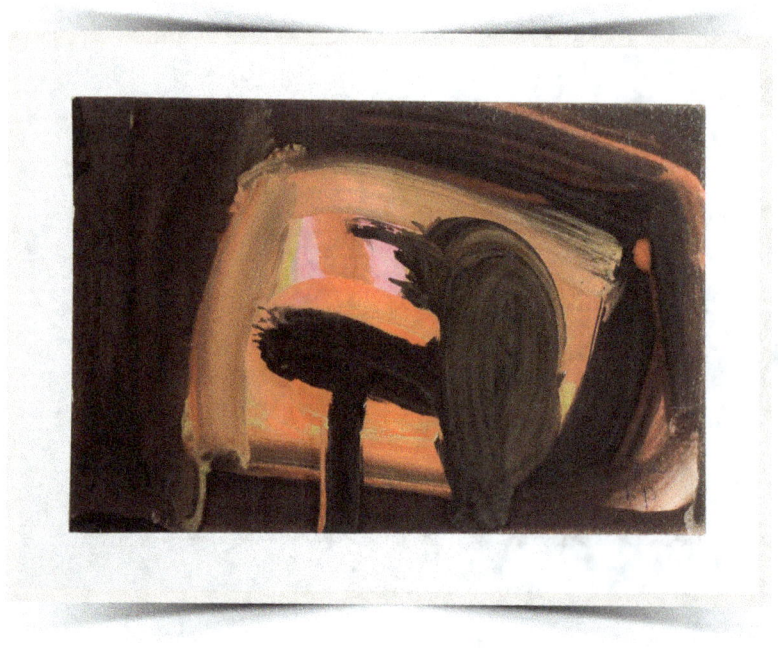

Tomorrow I will experiment.

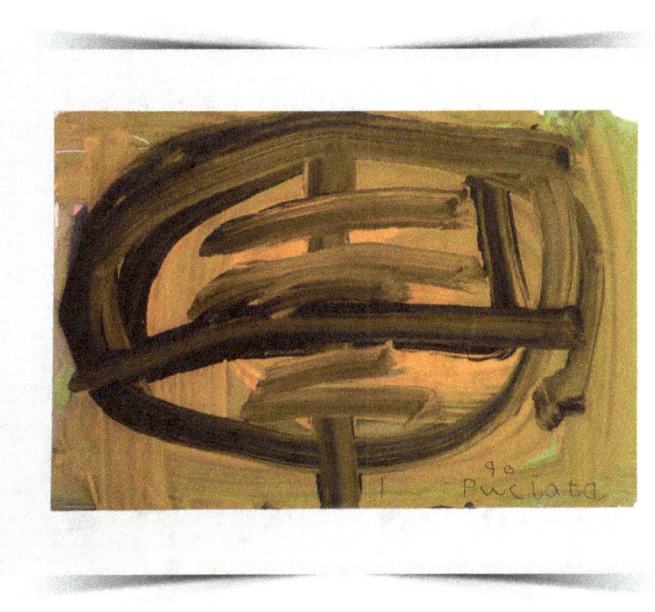

Why are there no women in the news?

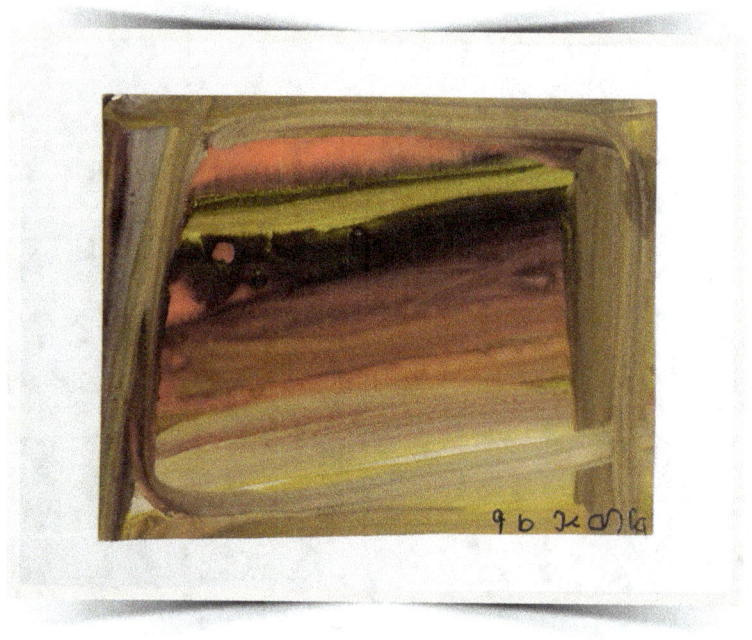

I need space to get some rest.

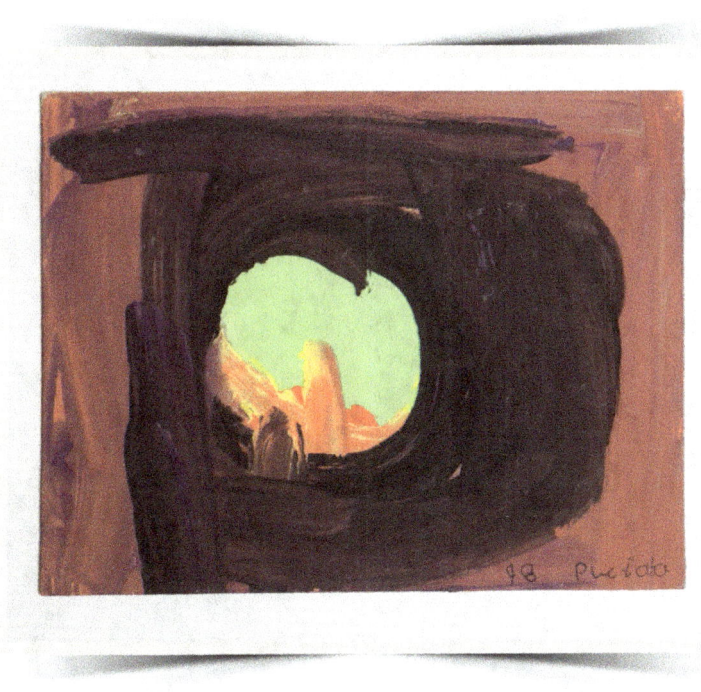

I feel very relaxed.

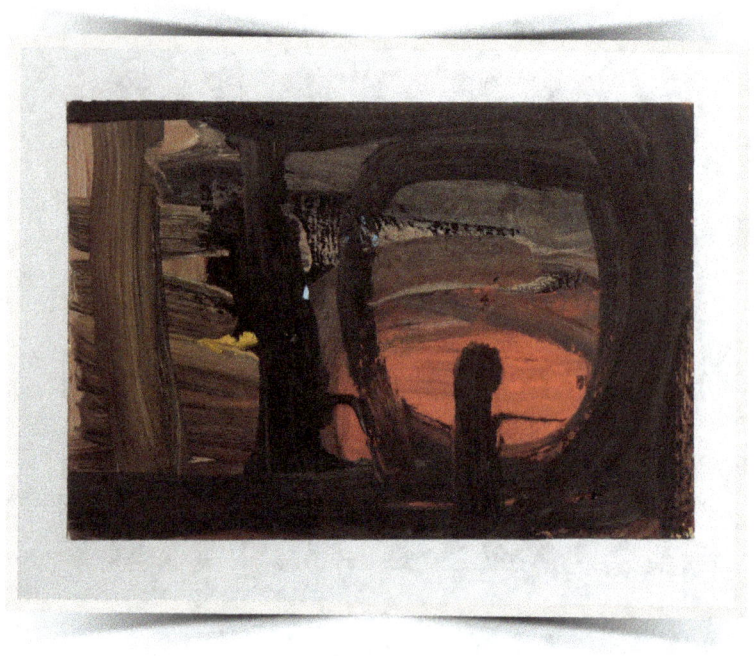

I will survive without school!

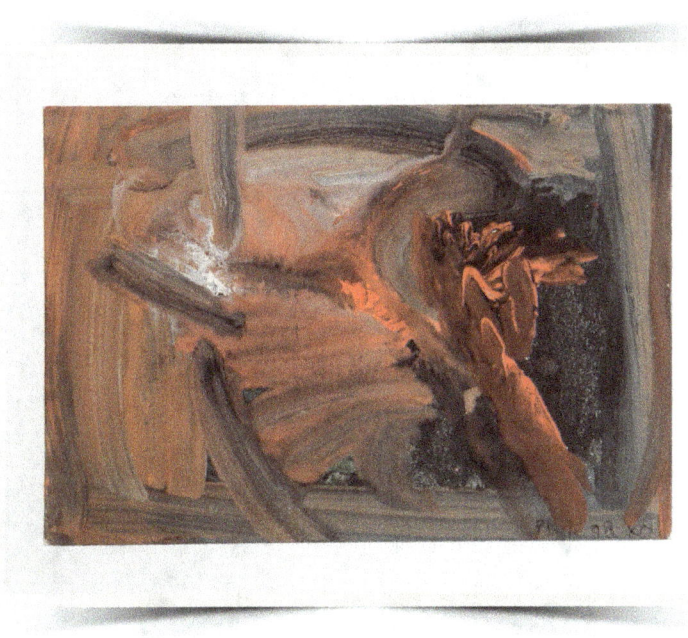

When Liniewski calls, tell him that I am cheating on him!

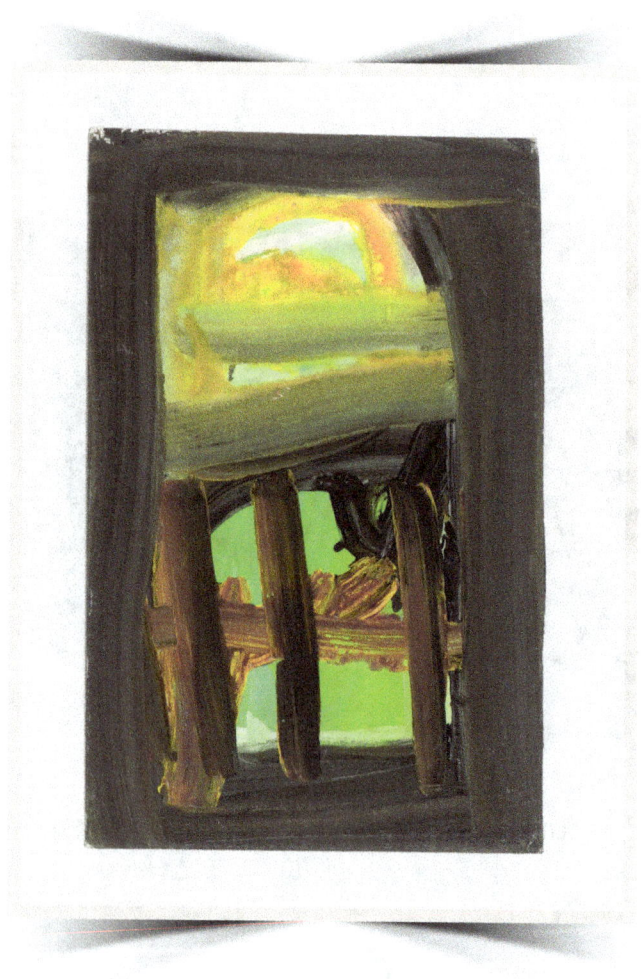

Are you going to miss me?

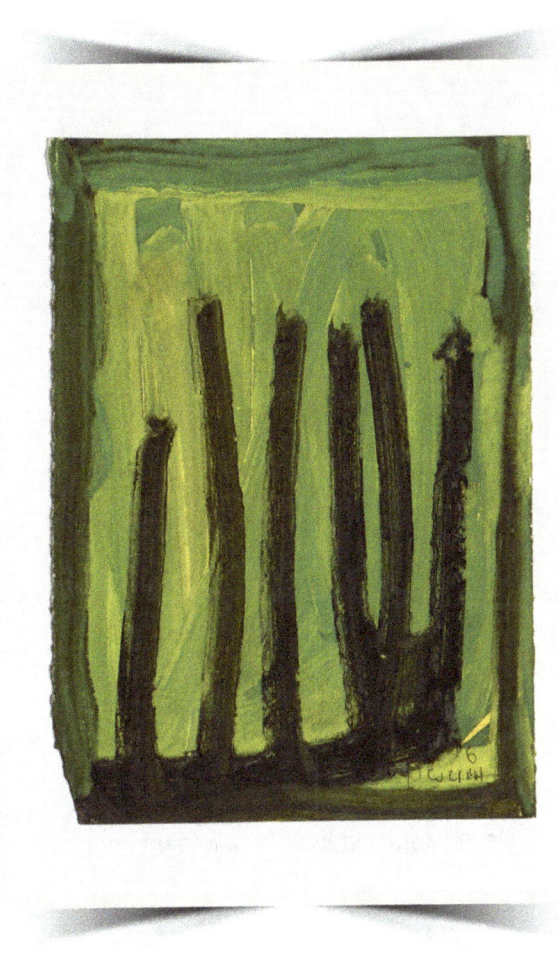

Why are you lonely, Mom?

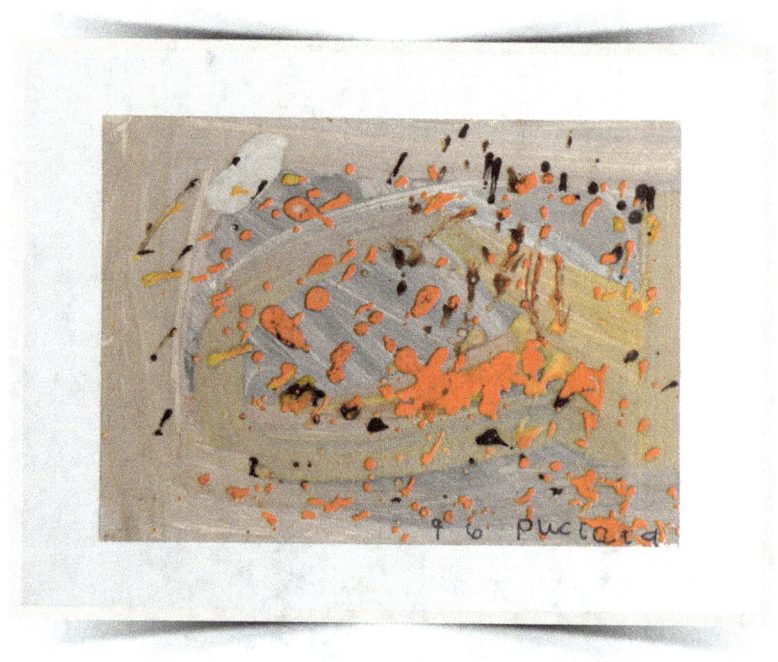

Doctor said you have to talk to me more!

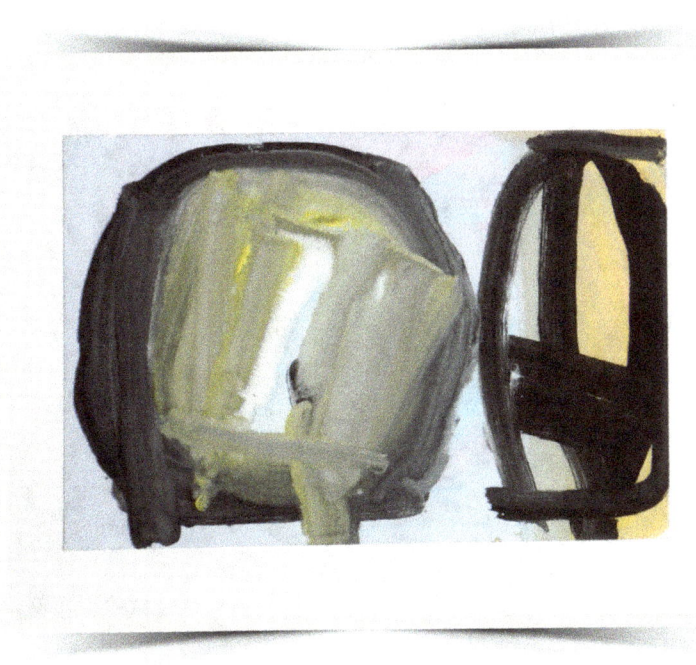

Mom, are you normal?

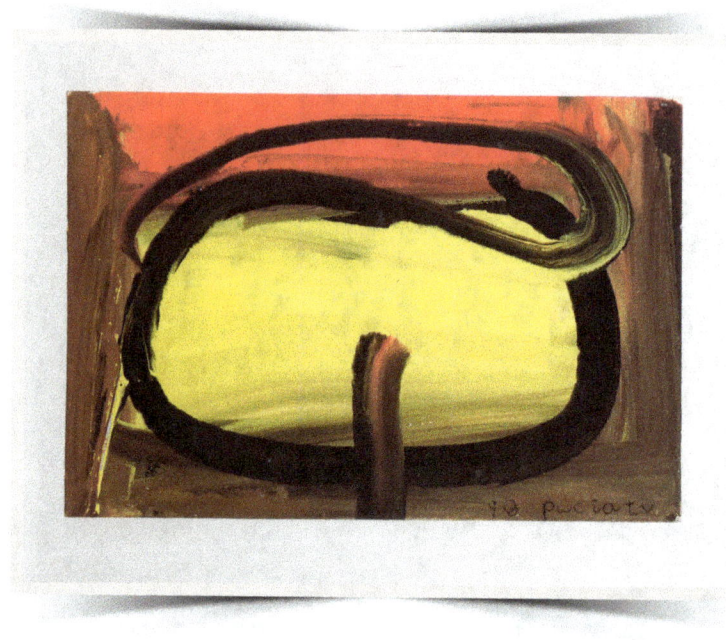

I talked to the doctor today and he was thrilled about me!

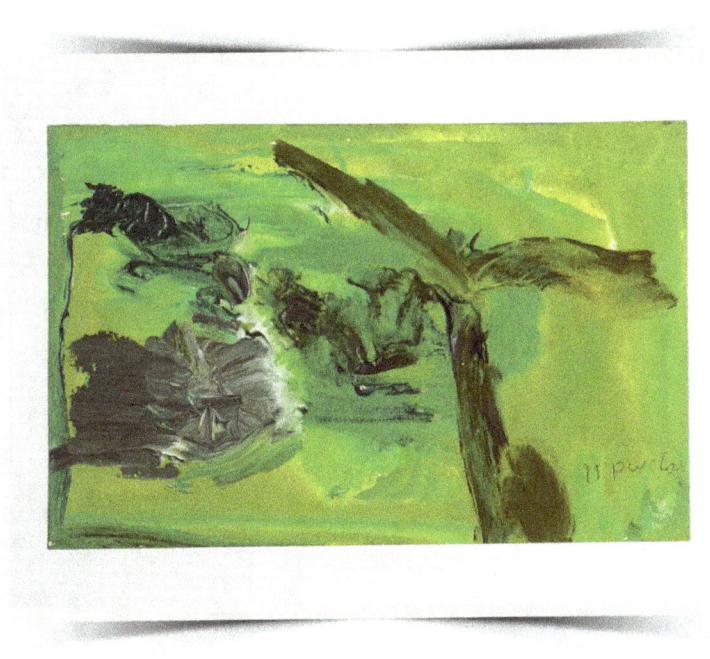

Today was a test for getting up from the bed.

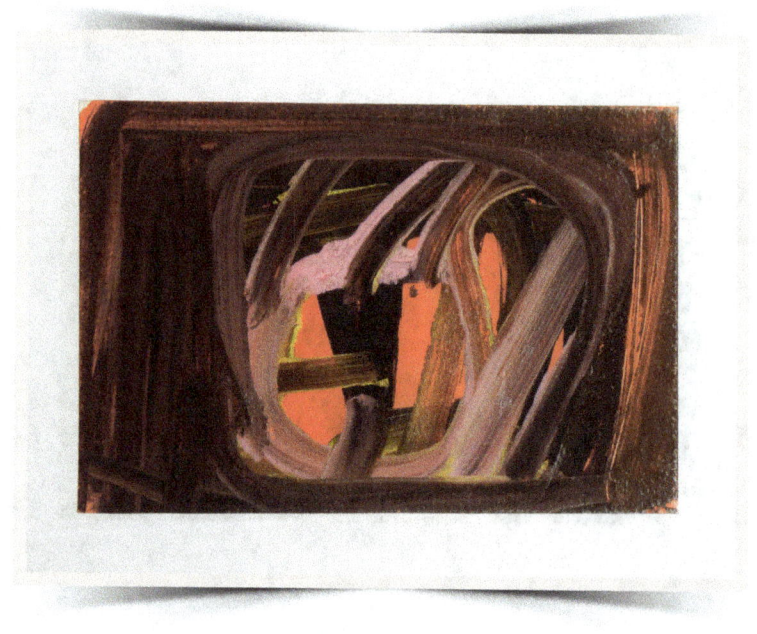

I am very sad today.

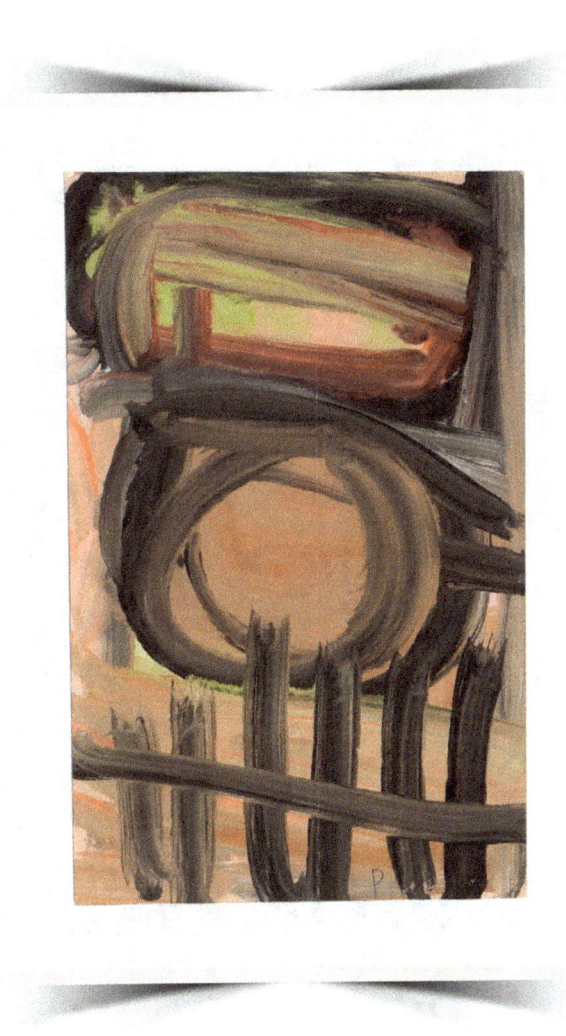

I am glad we are sitting at home today,
because I have a big problem going to school.

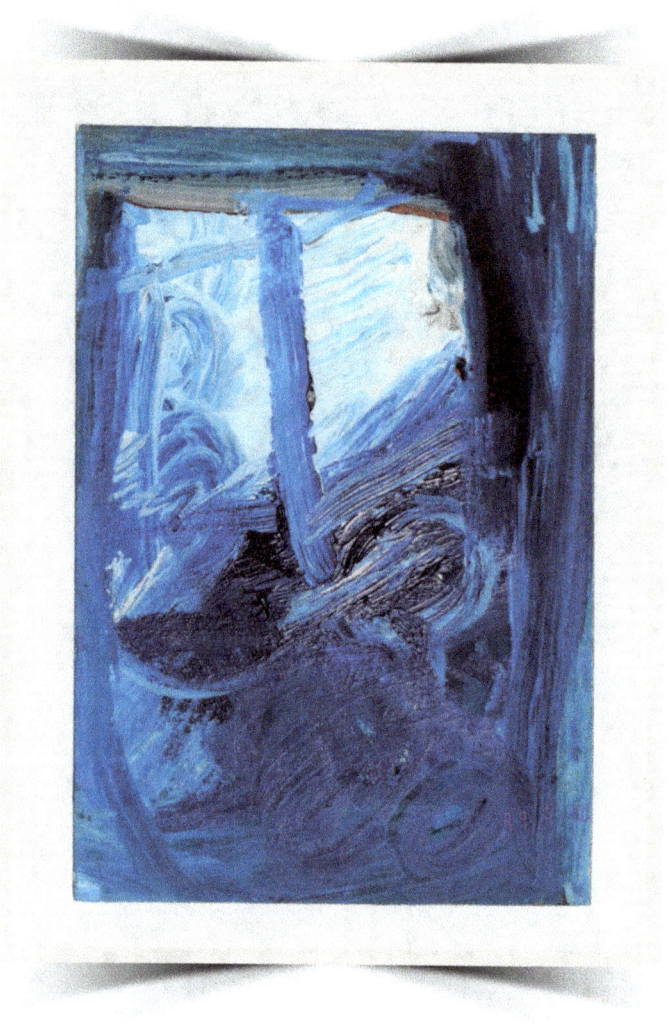

Mom is thinking, but she can't see anything.

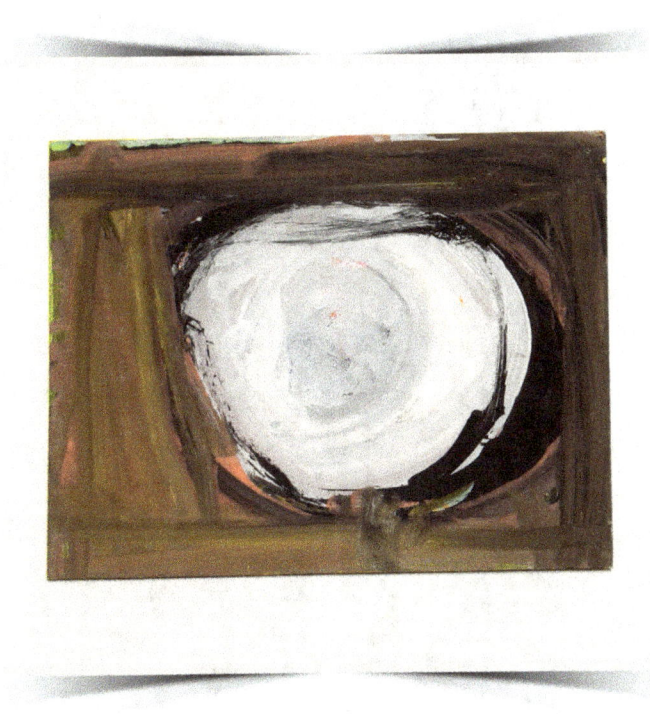

Dinner was a feast!

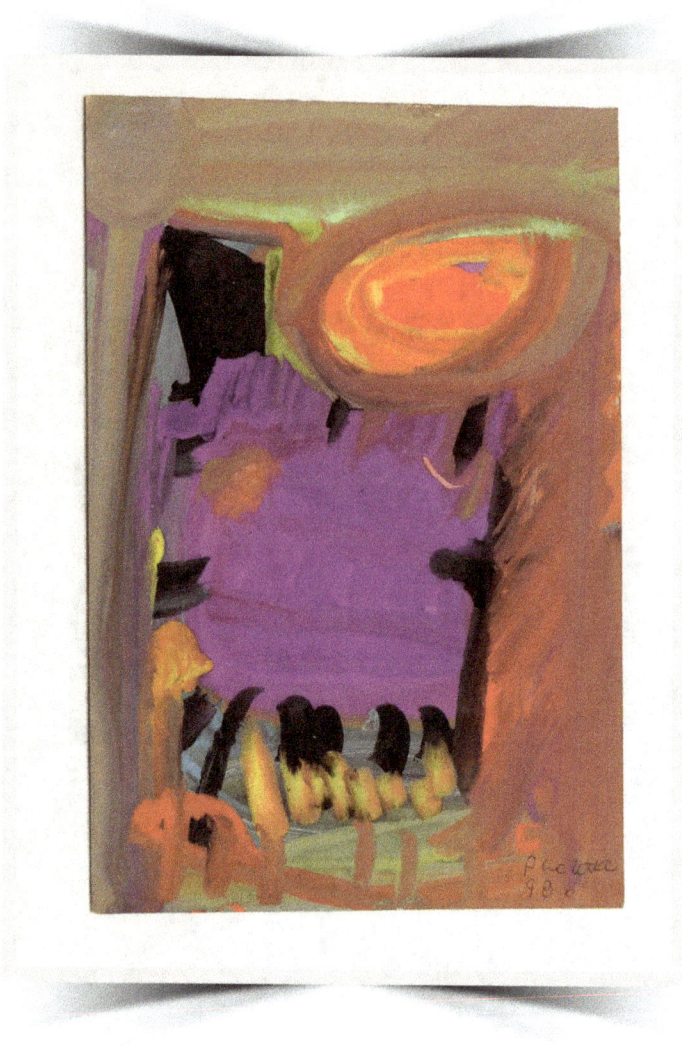

Speak to me in full sentences!

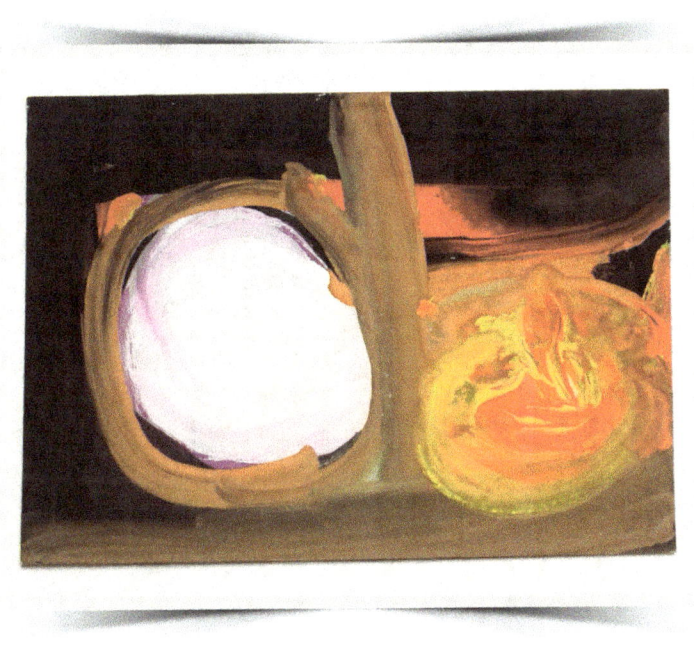

Today is a sad day.

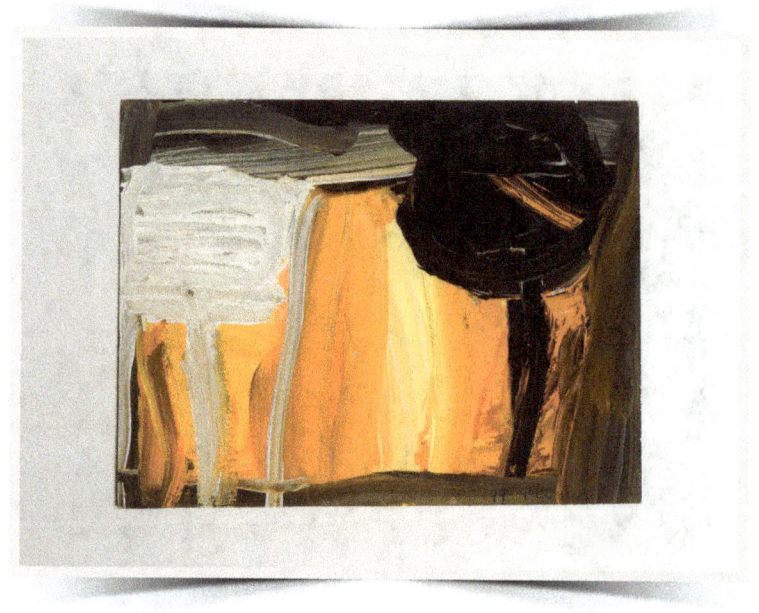

Mom, why did you get so old?

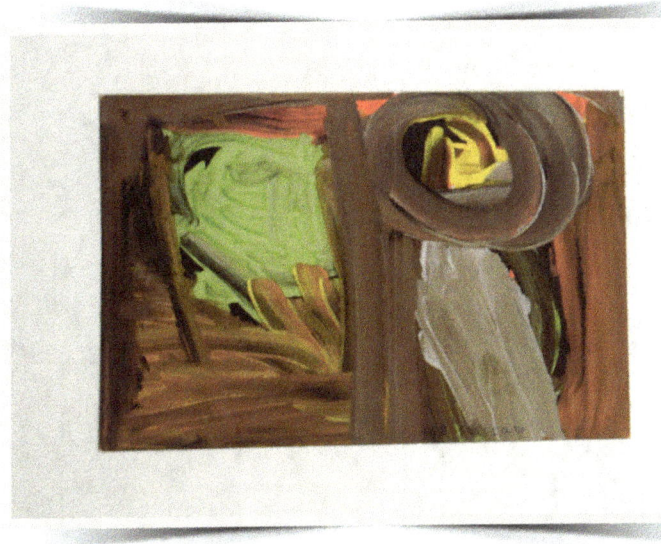

There are small rooms in Heaven, beds, two rooms and two beds. Who lives there? All that trust in His word. Not everyone will fit, and I won't have to go to school.

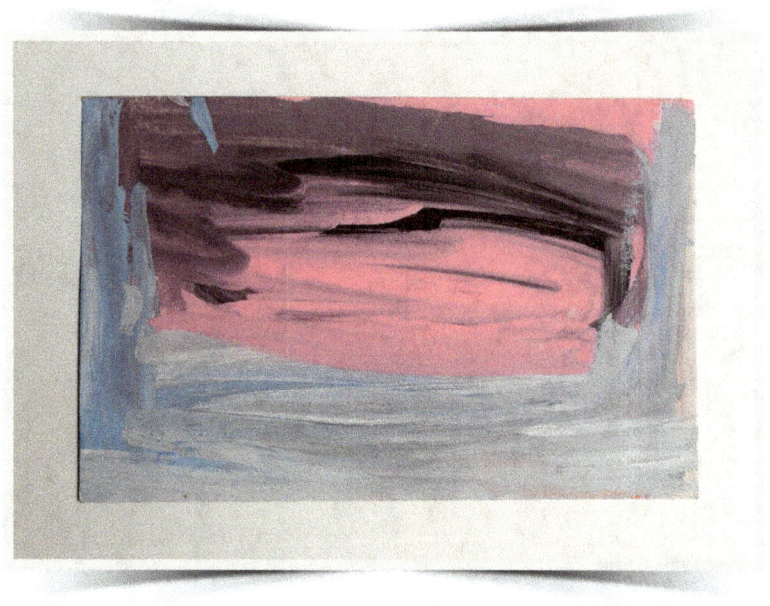

Mom sits so lonely.

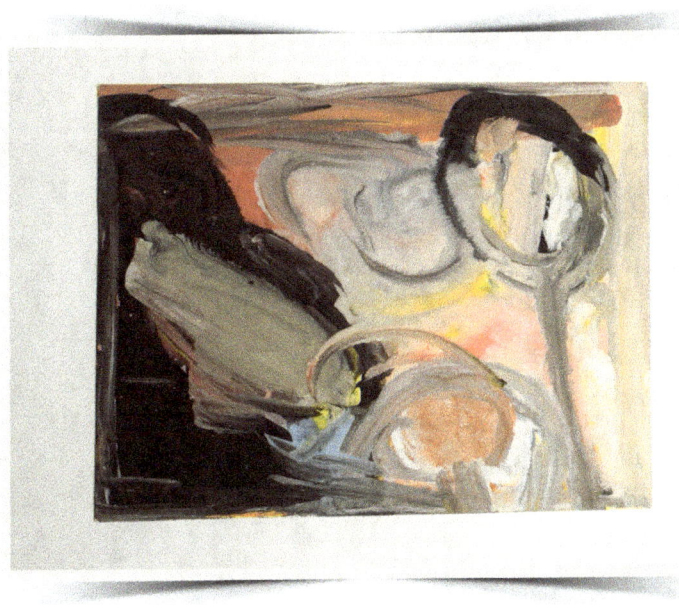

I am glad I didn't go to school today, because there is nothing at school. I can sit at home and take care of mom.

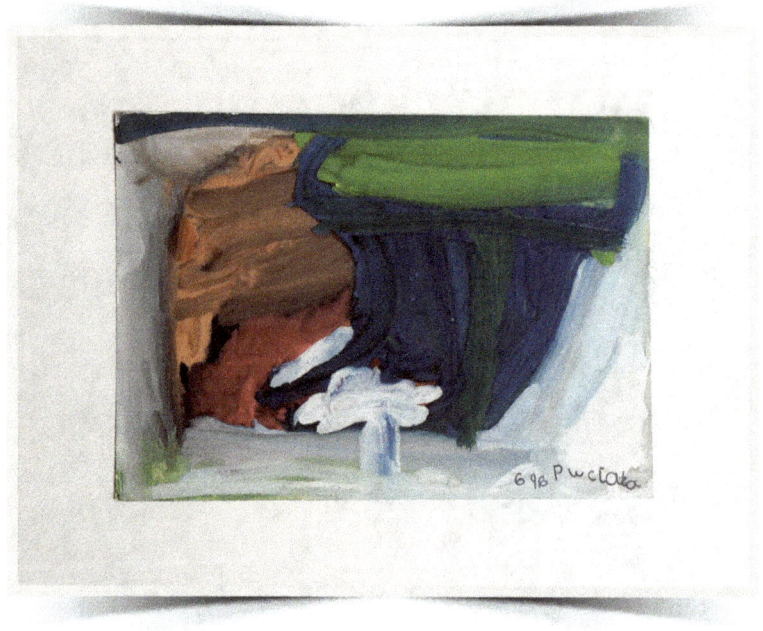

When is Joanna coming back? I think she's not.

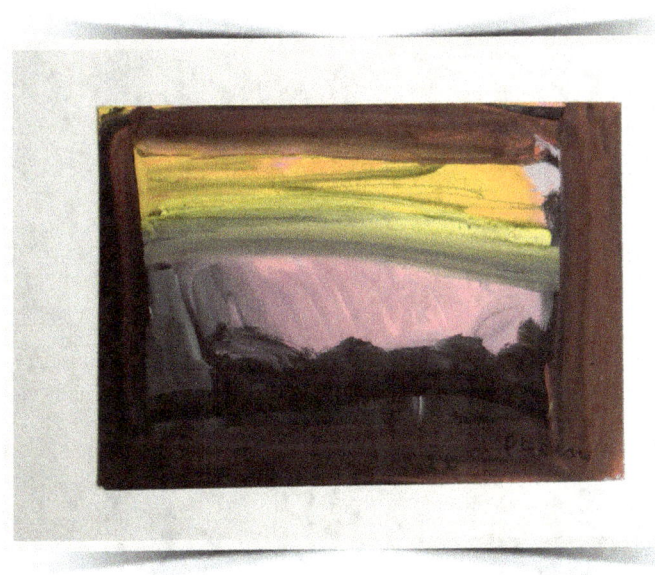

It's a good think I can talk.

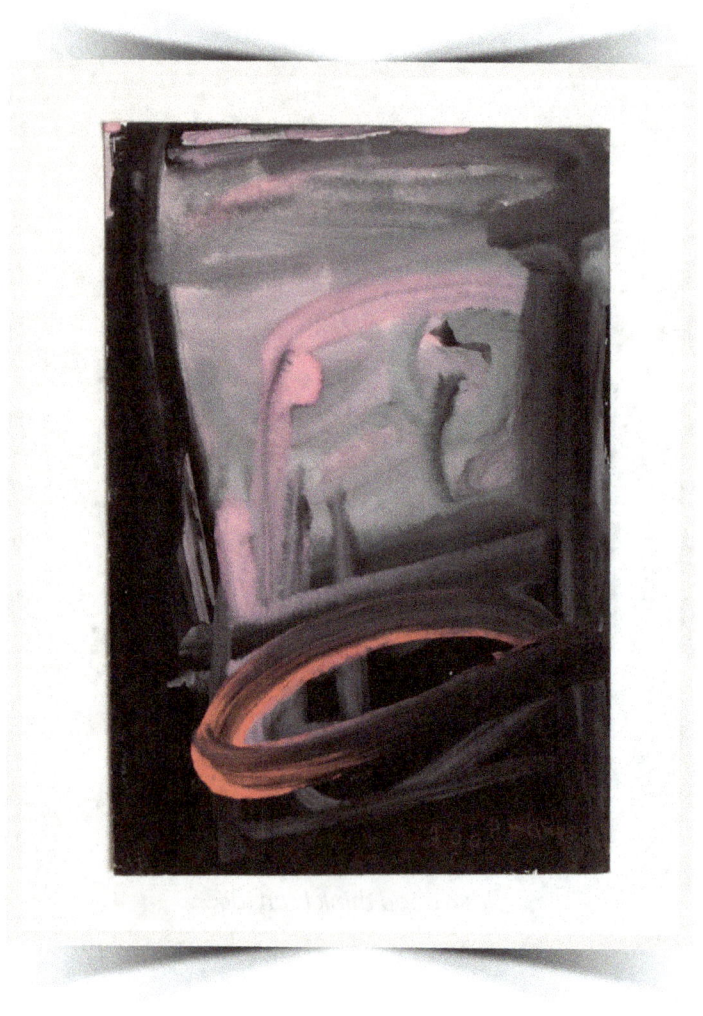

I am fat – I will not eat.

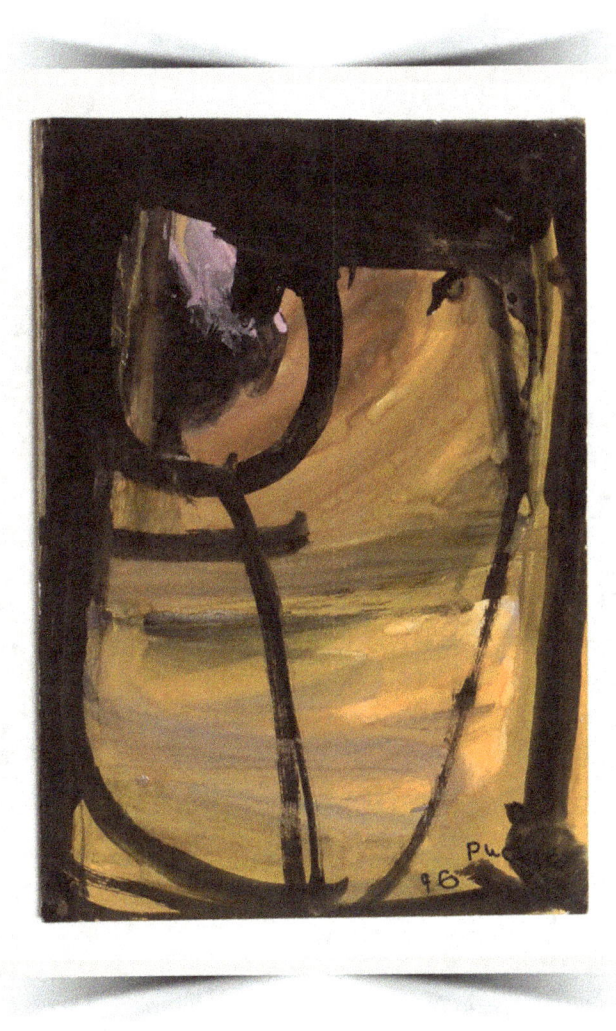

Why are you so aggressive?

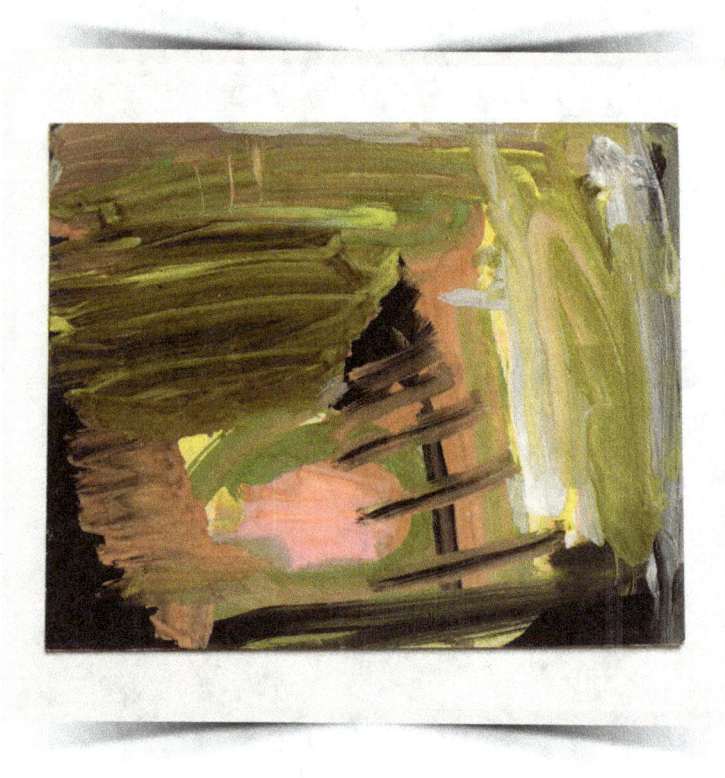

I am usually so crabby; it is hard for me to live.

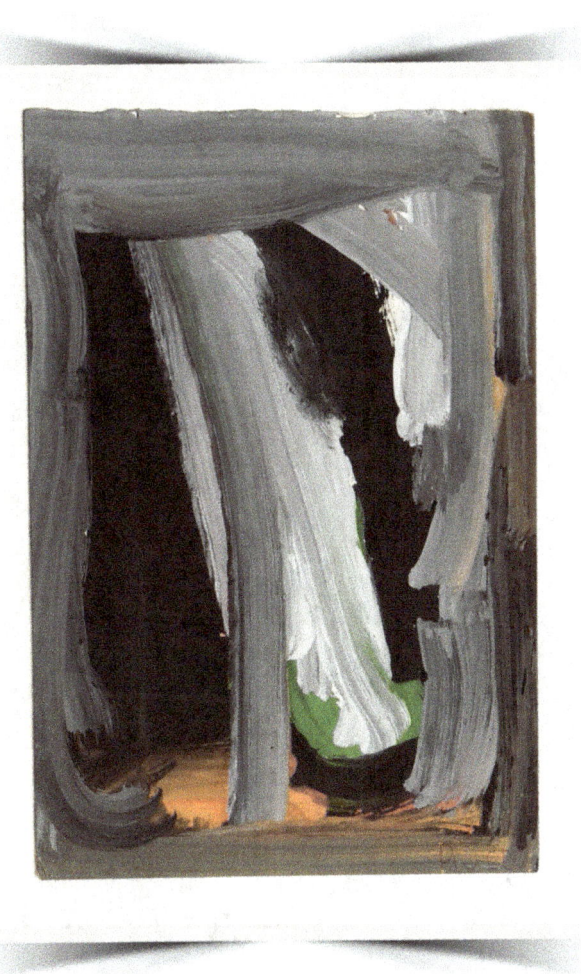

I will go to the other world. Why? Because I want to go there like so many other people do (talking about Heaven).

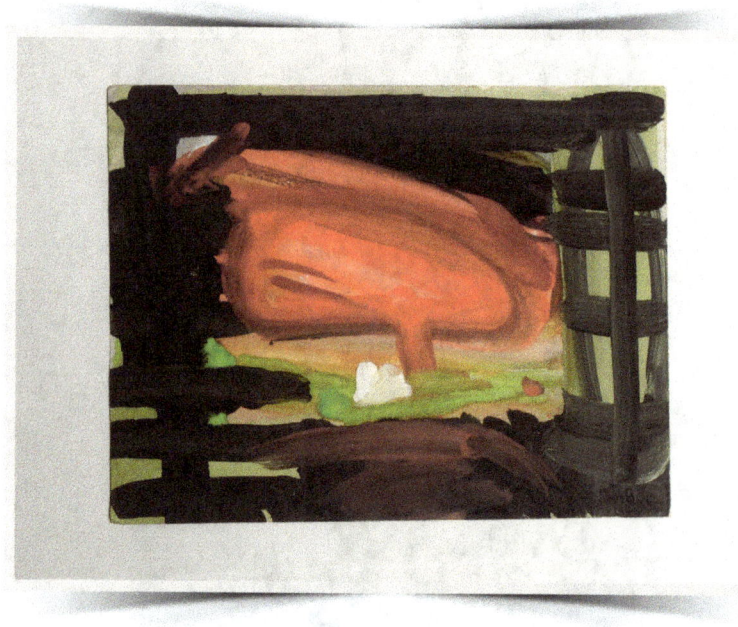

I would like to know when the world will end.
Will it end on Saturday, Tuesday or maybe Wednes-
day?
The priest says we don't know yet.

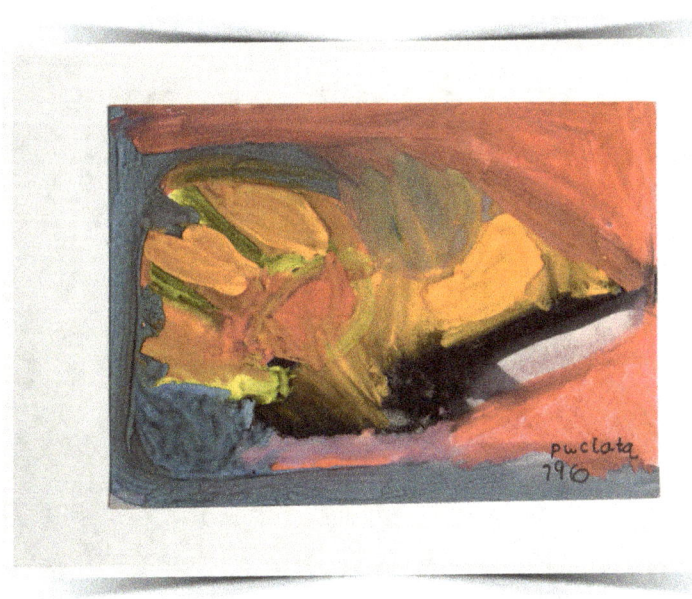

How do they burn in hell?

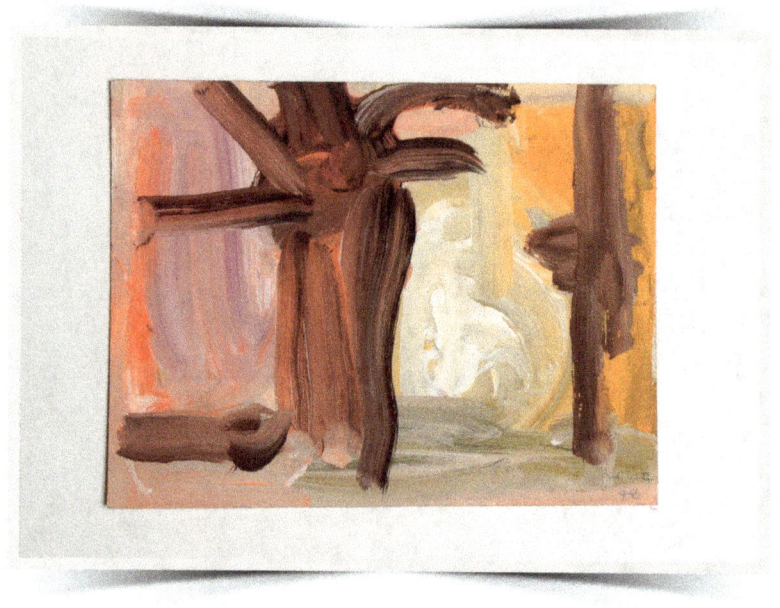

Do you die in your clothes?

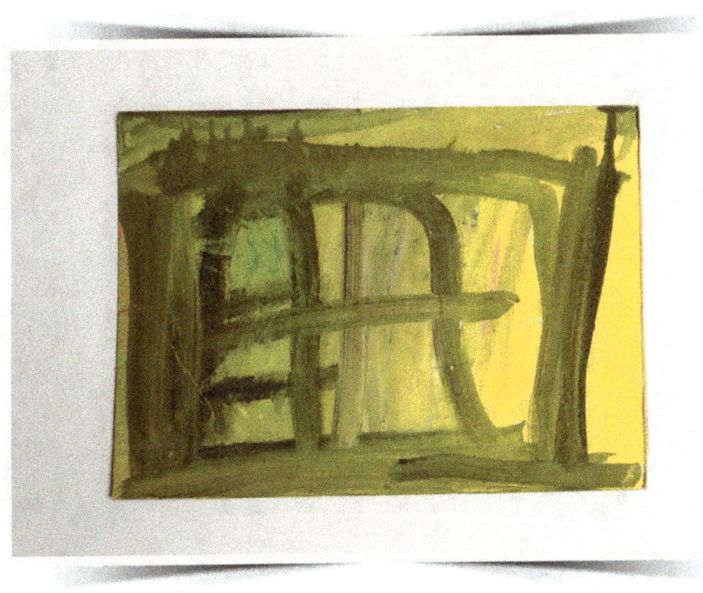

I don't want them to chop my brain!

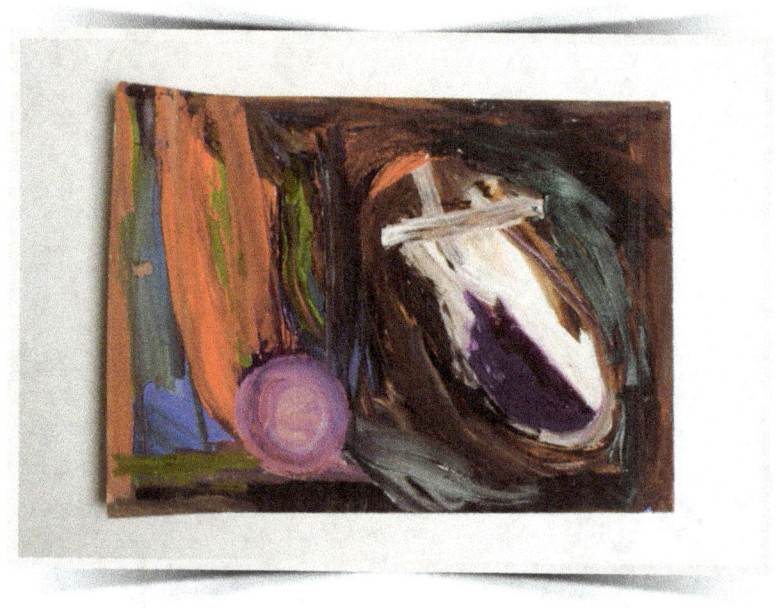

It is good in Heaven and miserable on Earth!

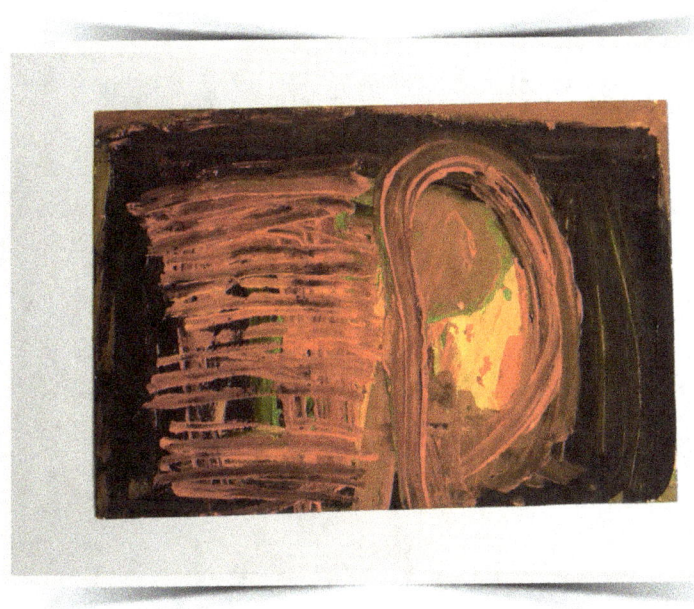

When one does not behave at school they are sent to a foster home. There they tie you up with safety belts and hit you. Foster home is a total disaster! I am happy I come from my own home.

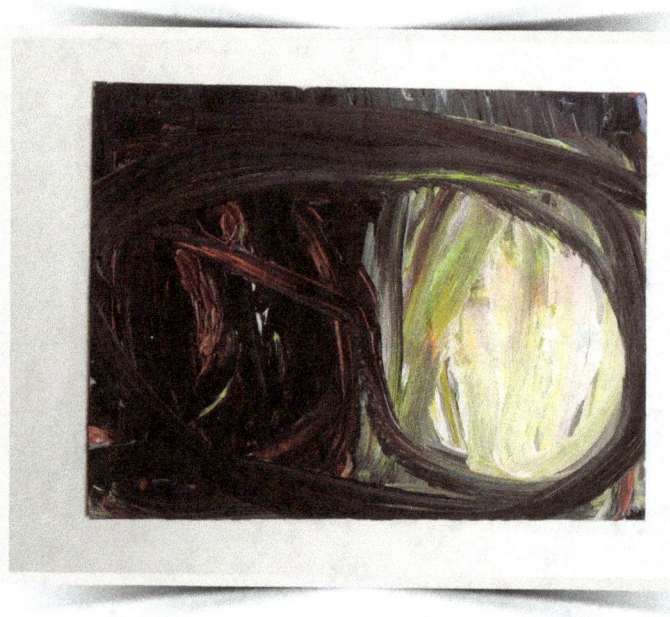

If I leave this world, there will only be me in
Heaven and the rest where will they be?
I know who will go to Heaven and who will go to Hell!

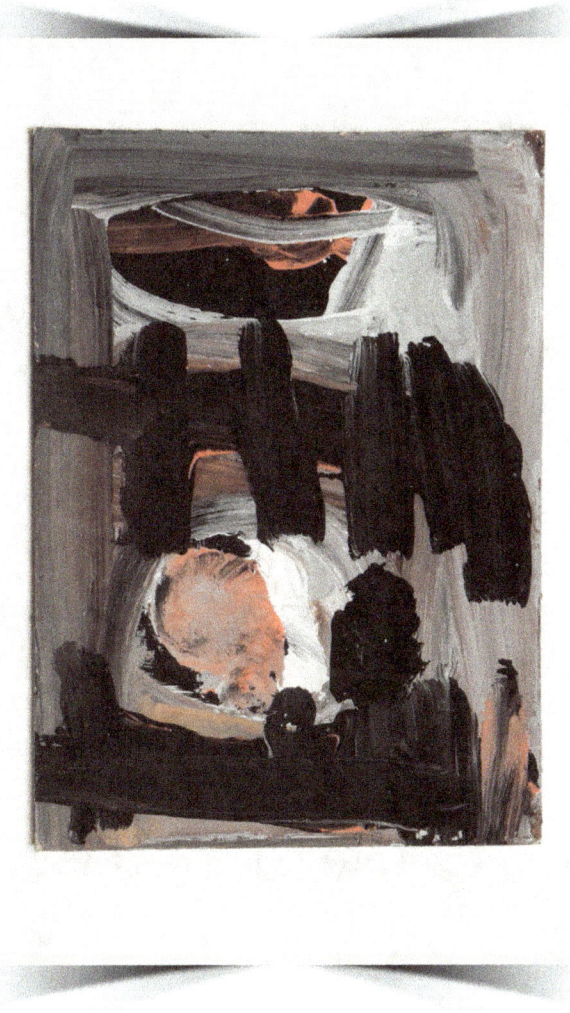

When everybody raises from their graves,
that's when I will contact God!

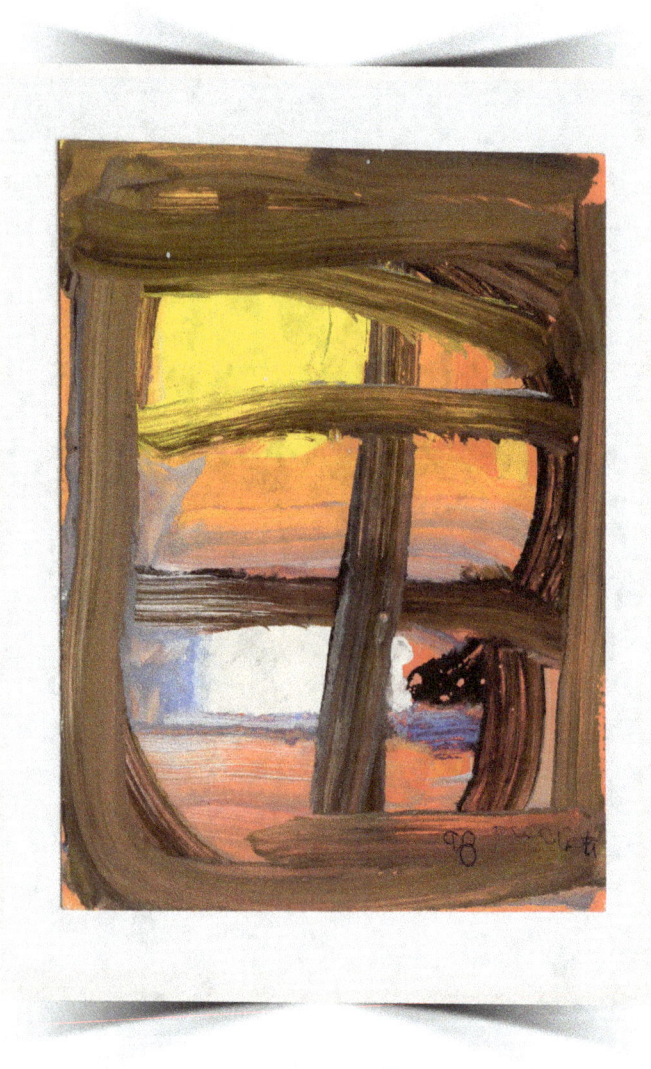

God will do confessions.

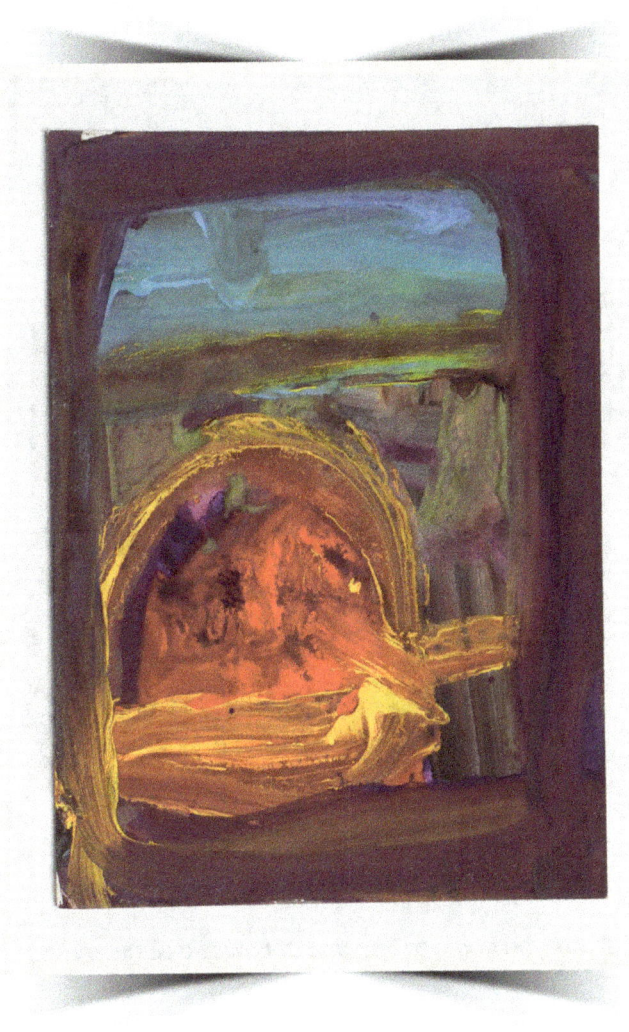

Will He have time to talk to me? Can one come to Him directly?

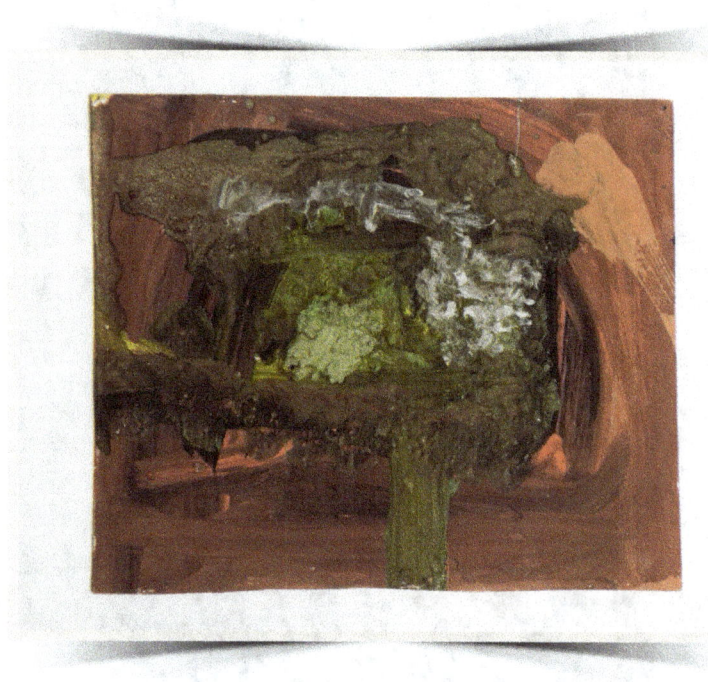

Are you going to bury me at Powazki cemetery?

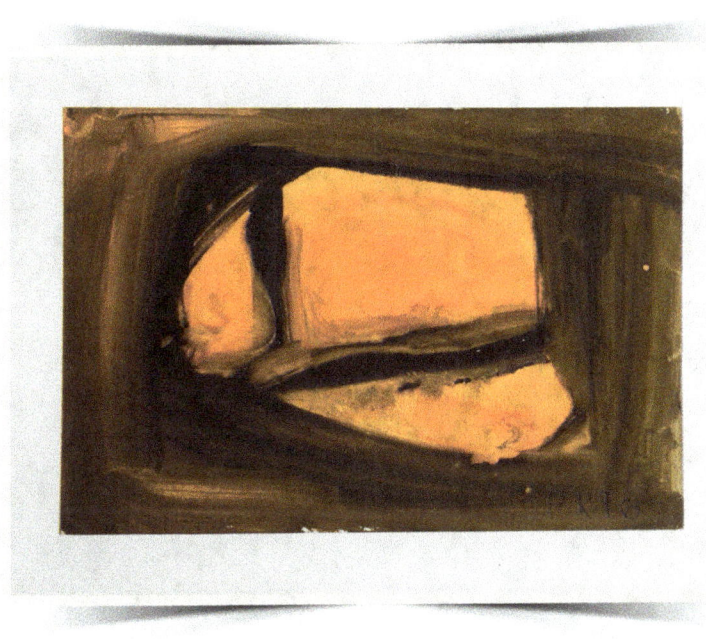

*Burry me in Powazki and cover me with soil,
like you covered Father.*

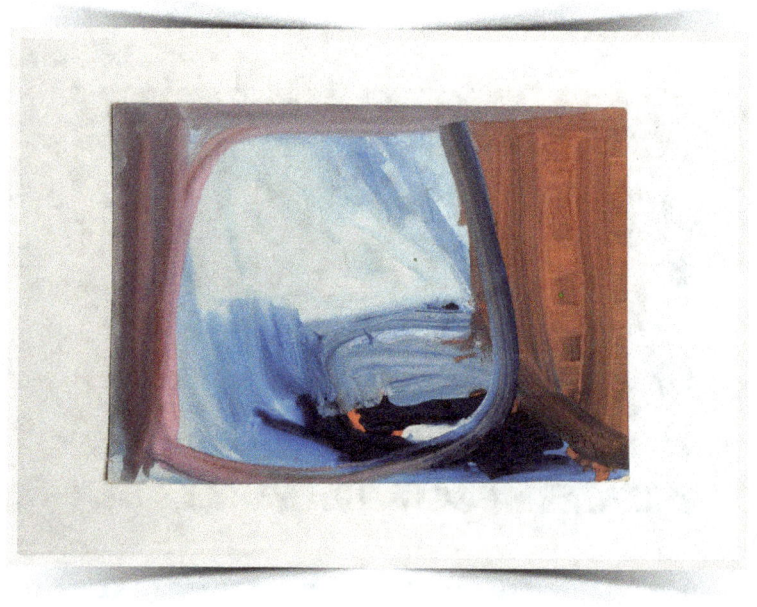

Why did God create the world?

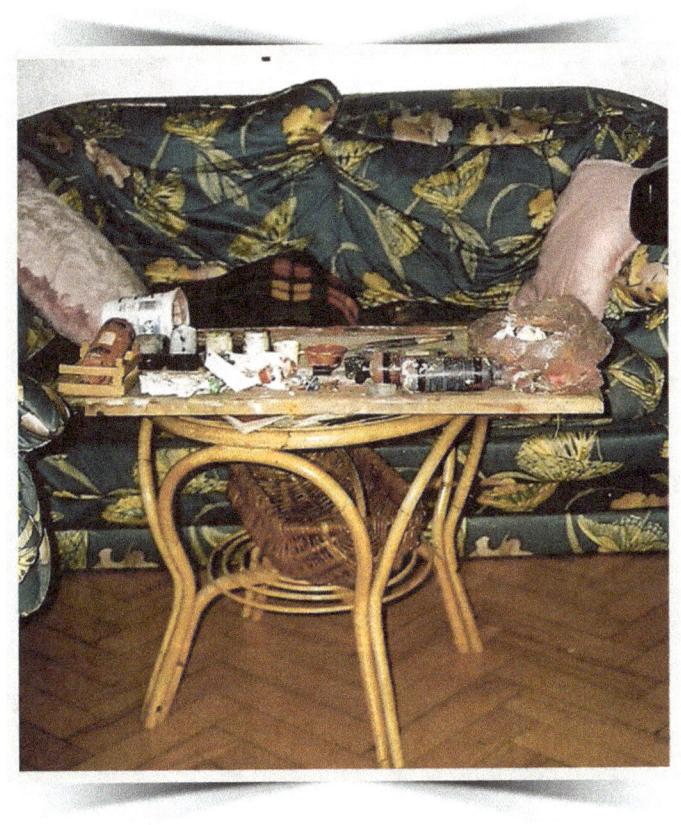

Just don't forget about me

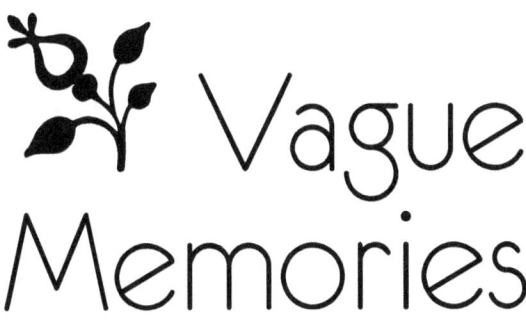

Vague
Memories

www.ingramcontent.com/pod-product-compliance
Lightning Source LLC
Chambersburg PA
CBHW071314220526
45468CB00001B/365